Social Media

A Selection of Addresses by
Hazrat Mirza Masroor Ahmad,
Khalifa tul Masih V (May Allah be his Helper)

Social Media

Issues Related to Social Media and its Resolution Proposed
by Hazrat Khalifatul-Masih V (May Allah be his Helper)

First Published in Urdu in the UK: 2018
(ISBN: 978-1-84880-186-8)

First English Translation Published in the USA April 2019
English Translation Complied by Lajna Imaillah USA
Translation by: Sadiqa Mian (USA Translation Team)
Under Supervision of ex. National President Lajna Imaillah USA
Saliha Malik (2010-2018)
Revised Edition English Translation Published in UK June 2019
Published by:
Lajna Section Markazia
22 Deer Park Road, SW19 3TL, London

© Islam International Publications Limited

Printed in the UK at:
Raqeem Press, Farnham

Cover Design by: Musawer Ahmad Din

ISBN: 978-1-84880-934-5

Objective of Human Creation

وَ مَا خَلَقْتُ الْجِنَّ وَ الْإِنْسَ إِلَّا لِيَعْبُدُوْنِ ۞

'**And I have not created the Jinn and the men but that they may worship Me.**' (Holy Quran 51:57)

Foreword

Social Media can lead to benefits and harms; hence, our Lajna and Nasirat should use it with caution. In this book, Lajna Markazia (Central) has compiled the instructions that I have given on this topic at various occasions. All of you should try to act on it.

May Allah enable you to do this. Ameen.

Mirza Masroor Ahmad
Khalifatul Masih V

Hazrat Mirza Masroor Ahmad
Khalifatul Masih V

Introduction

In the current times, we are benefiting from the fast progress made through latest technology and communication systems, which provides many benefits at a global level: instant communication, expression of opinion and knowledge sharing through Social Media. However, a bitter reality is also evident that the irresponsible use of Social Media has led to moral weaknesses at a personal and societal level.

Lajna Markazia (Central) is honored to compile this book on the topic of "Social Media" as a directive from Hazrat Khalifatul Masih V [aba] [May Allah be his Helper]. This book is a compilation of wisdom filled guidance and beautiful exhortations from Friday sermons, addresses, messages and question and answer sessions from the beginning of Fifth Khilafat till 2017. Alhamdollilah-e-Zalik [All praise belongs to Allah for this]. We pray to Allah the Almighty to accept this effort and may it be a guiding light for the readers of this book. Ameen.

Respected Rizwana Nisar Sahiba (Muavina Lajna Section Markazia) devotedly worked hard through all stages of gathering, selecting and compiling of addresses and exhortations. Respected Mahmood Ahmad Malik Sahib (Life Devotee - Worker Additional Wakalat Publication, London) provided guidance and support throughout. May Allah bless them the best reward in this world and hereafter.

Humbly,
Rehana Ahmad
In charge, Lajna Section Markazia

Table of Contents

****

Objective of Human Creation

- Objective of Human Creation
- Excessive use of TV and Internet leads to Neglect of Worship

Objective of Human Creation

What is the objective of human creation? What does it demand and how can one achieve the purpose of life? Hazrat Khalifatul Masih V (aba) has elaborated on this topic in many Friday sermons and addresses. In a Friday sermon, instructing the members of the Jama'at, he (aba) said:

"Allah the Almighty has bestowed a huge favor on man that He exalted him above all other creations and granted him a mind that allows him to subjugate other living beings and things created by God, and take maximum advantage of those. Each day the human mind is using this faculty to bring forth the latest innovations. The worldly progress today was not seen ten years ago, and worldly progress seen ten years ago was not seen twenty years ago. As we keep looking back [in time], we can appreciate the importance of the latest innovations and the capability of the human mind. However, is the material progress achieved by man the objective of his life? Throughout history, worldly man considered the objective of life to be attainment of progress, power, worldly grandeur, might, and indulgence in worldly luxuries and exuberances using his wealth to establish his superiority over the less fortunate, using his wealth to gain physical comfort and using his power to subjugate others. An ordinary worldly man who does not have wealth thinks the same way. Young men of today who are not drawn to religion and are engrossed in the world think that these latest inventions, such as television and Internet, are the real means to progress and are greatly influenced by such things. This is an extremely erroneous concept. This concept has created greater tyrants. This concept has created most cruel individuals. This concept has created many men, who are engrossed in hedonism. Each era has seen Pharaohs created by this idea because of their power, wealth, might and grandeur. Allah the Almighty, who is the Lord of the worlds and the Creator of all the worlds, has strongly refuted this concept. He said, what you consider to be the objective of your life is not! You were not created so that you may gain benefit from the material things and then leave this world. No! Instead Allah the Almighty said:

وَ مَا خَلَقْتُ الْجِنَّ وَ الْإِنْسَ اِلَّا لِيَعْبُدُوْنِ ٥

'And I have not created the Jinn and the men but that they may worship Me.' (Holy Quran 51:57)"

- Friday Sermon delivered 15 January 2010 at Baitul Futuh Mosque, London.
- Published AlFazl International 05 February 2010

Excessive use of TV and Internet leads to Neglect of Worship

In a Friday sermon Huzoor-e-Anwar (Beloved Huzoor) (aba) recited Tashahhud, Ta'awwuz and Surah Fātiḥah and then recited the following verse of Sura An-Nur and explained its translation:

يَا اَيُّهَا الَّذِيْنَ اٰمَنُوْا لَا تَتَّبِعُوْا خُطُوٰتِ الشَّيْطٰنِ ۙ وَ مَنْ يَّتَّبِعْ خُطُوٰتِ الشَّيْطٰنِ فَاِنَّهٗ يَأْمُرُ بِالْفَحْشَاءِ وَ الْمُنْكَرِ ۚ وَ لَوْ لَا فَضْلُ اللّٰهِ عَلَيْكُمْ وَ رَحْمَتُهٗ مَا زَكٰى مِنْكُمْ مِّنْ اَحَدٍ اَبَدًا ۙ وَّ لٰكِنَّ اللّٰهَ يُزَكِّيْ مَنْ يَّشَاءُ ۚ وَ اللّٰهُ سَمِيْعٌ عَلِيْمٌ ٥

O ye who believe! follow not the footsteps of Satan, and whoso follows the footsteps of Satan should know that he surely enjoins immorality and manifest evil. And but for the grace of Allah and His mercy upon you, not one of you would ever be pure, but Allah purifies whom He pleases. And Allah is All-Hearing, All-Knowing. (Holy Quran, 24:22)

Huzoor-e-Anwar (aba) then used this verse to discuss those matters that hinder a man from reaching the objective of his life (i.e. worshiping his Creator). Huzoor-e-Anwar (aba) said:

"It is important to erect defenses against Satan in our homes that not only protect us from each attack but are also able to launch a counter attack.Do not let Satan enter your life by accepting his love as [true] love. Instead, each Ahmadi should make effort to seek Allah's protection by doing Istighfār (repentance) all the time. Allah the Exalted is the greatest defense against Satan. Thus, in this world gone astray, one should seek protection from Allah by doing Istighfār because Istighfār is the only way to come under the protection of Allah.

No human knowingly approaches evil. It is against human nature to do something that one knows will lead to harm. Allah the Exalted has clearly explained the good and the evil to a true believer. One should identify good and evil according to the teachings of Allah the Exalted and should act or abstain accordingly. Satan knows that he cannot harm a man who is in the protection and fort of Allah the Exalted. Therefore, Satan takes a man out of this protection and takes him out of the fort of Allah and makes man follow him. It is obvious that to take a man out of Allah's protection, he tempts him with virtuous deeds. Or one can say that a believer can only be taken out of the protection of Allah by giving him the temptation of good deeds."

Huzoor (aba) then said:

"Evils of these days include television and the Internet. You can observe this in most homes that the eldest to the youngest are not offering Fajr Salat on time as they were either watching TV or were online on the Internet until late, watching some program and, as a result, they could not wake up on time. In fact, such people do not even realize that they have to get up for Salat in the morning. Both the Internet and TV and similar useless things not only cause you to miss your Salat once or twice, but those who fall victim to this behavior get into this habit of watching programs until late at night or sitting on the Internet. Then it becomes difficult to get up for the prayer in the morning and [such people] may not even wake up [at a reasonable time]. Some people eventually fail to give any importance to Salat.

Salat is a fundamental obligation; its observance is necessary in all circumstances, even in war, difficulty and sickness. It must be offered even if a person has to offer Salat sitting, lying down, or in the case of war or travel offer it as qasr (reduced form). But it must be offered. In ordinary circumstances, men are directed to offer it in congregation and women are also directed to offer it on time. However, Satan diverts a person away from Salat for the sake of a single worldly program. Additionally, Internet is such that it continues to engage one in the various programs and applications using a phone or iPad. At first, good programs are watched on these. Its attraction is such that, at first good programs are watched, then all kinds of filthy and destructive immoral programs are watched, which destroy morality. There is restlessness in many homes because the rights of wives are not taken care of and children's rights are not fulfilled because men are busy watching vulgar programs on TV and Internet during the night. Consequently, the children of these homes are colored in the same hue, and they watch the same. Hence, an Ahmadi house should try to stay clear of all these ills.

The Holy Prophet (sallaho alaihe wassalam [saw] May peace and blessings of Allah be on him) was so concerned about saving the believers from the attacks of Satan that he [saw] taught his companions prayers to save them from Satan, and he taught them comprehensive prayers. A companion has narrated that he (saw) taught us this prayer:

'O Allah create love in our hearts, reform us, and make us tread upon the paths of security, and take us to light saving us from darkness, and save us from overt and covert indecencies, and place blessings for us in our ears, in our eyes, in our hearts, in our wives and in our children, and turn to us with mercy. You are the acceptor of repentance and the one who forgives time and again. Make us the ones who are grateful for your favors and appreciate them and accept

them. And, O Allah, perfect Your favors on us.'
(Sunnan Abu Daud Kitabus Salat. Bab Al-Tashahud Hadith 969)

Thus, this is the prayer to restrain from wrong worldly entertainment"

- Friday Sermon delivered 20 May 2016 at Gottenberg Mosque, Sweden
- Published AlFazl International 10 June 2016

In addition to the Friday sermons, on many occasions Huzoor (aba) has explained that excessive use of technology is a hindrance to worship. In a Waqf-e-nau class, he (aba) explained:
"If you have fear of Allah the Exalted, then you will have love for Him, as well. Allah the Exalted says that if you take one step towards me, I will take two steps [towards you] and if one comes to me walking, I will go to him running"
Huzoor-e-Anwar (aba) then said:
"If the worldly desire increases so that one is engrossed in TV dramas and the Internet and is late in offering Salat, then love for Allah cannot develop. Gaining this love requires sacrifice of desires."

- Waqfe Nau Class 08 October 2011 at Masjid Baitur Rasheed Germany
- Published AlFazl International 06 January 2012

In a Friday sermon, Huzoor (aba) drew attention of the Ahmadis towards increasing their overt morals and fulfilling the rights of Allah. He said:
"After coming to the Western countries and under the influence of the worldly society, some people have become too involved in worldliness. Though they verbally claim to give precedence to faith over all worldly things, however, in reality their practice is contrary to it. The Ahmadis here are very good at integrating with the local population and showing good morals to those outside [our community] but their standards of worship

and fulfilling the rights of Allah the Almighty are not what is expected from an Ahmadi…"

Referencing the sayings of the Promised Messiah (alaihesalam [as] May peace be on him), Huzoor (aba) highlighted some moral weakness that should be removed. He also advised against inappropriate use of the latest inventions of modern times, avoiding gatherings where there is shirk (associating partners with Allah) and giving precedence to faith over worldly matters. Huzoor (aba) said:

"Promised Messiah (as) repeatedly reminded his community about how they should transform and what the condition of their faith should be. In this context, I want to present an excerpt so that each one of us becomes the one fulfilling the demands of the Bai'at (pledge of allegiance). Giving his community an important instruction, he (as) said:

'Corruption is growing in this age and every kind of idolatry, innovation and evil is spreading. When at the time of Bai'at, you pledge to give preference to the faith over the world, it is a pledge you make before God.' Think about it as if the pledge was made in front of God. 'You must remain steadfast upon it till your death. Otherwise, you have not pledged Bai'at. But if you do remain steadfast, then God will bless you both in the faith and in the world.'

He (as) says, 'In keeping with God's will, you should adopt Taqwa to the fullest extent. The time is perilous and the signs of Divine wrath are becoming manifest. Whoever changes himself, according to the Will of God, will do an act of mercy for his own self, his family and his children.' The current situation in the world is constantly deteriorating. In view of the state of the world, everyone should turn towards God. He (as) says: "There are two kinds of evil. One is to associate partners with God and to not recognize His Greatness and be lazy in His worship and obedience. The second is not showing benevolence to His people and not fulfilling their rights. It should be that neither of these transgressions are committed. Be obedient to God. Stay

steadfast on the pledge of allegiance that you have taken. Do not cause pain to God's people. Read the Holy Quran attentively. Act on it. Avoid all kinds of raucous and vulgar talk and polytheistic gatherings. Establish five daily prayers. Hence, you should not ignore any of the commandments of Allah. Keep your body clean and keep your heart clean of any excessive meanness, malice and jealousy. These are the things that Allah wants from you."
{Malfoozat volume 5 page 75 to 76 Edition 1985 published in England}

After reading this saying of Promised Messiah (as), Huzoor-e-Anwar (aba) said:

"Now all of us need to analyze ourselves as to what extent we have safeguarded ourselves from vulgar and polytheistic gatherings. There are many who would say that they believe in one God and do not sit in polytheistic gatherings. **However, remember that any activity such as Internet or TV or any act or gathering that makes you neglect your prayers and worship is an polytheistic gathering.**"

- Friday Sermon delivered 21 April 2017 at Frankfurt, Germany
- Published AlFazl International 12 May 2017

Inappropriate use of Social Media affects the standard of worship and acceptance of prayers, in a Friday sermon Huzoor-e-Anwar (aba) explained this by citing a saying of the Promised Messiah (as). Huzoor-e-Anwar said:

"At one place, the Promised Messiah (as) said:'When prayers are made with complete devotion to God, they bring about extraordinary effect. It should be remembered that acceptance of prayers is by God alone and there is an appointed time for prayers. Just as morning is a special time and the distinction of morning is not shared by any other hour. Similarly, there are certain times which generate acceptance and effect in prayer."
{Malfoozat Volume 4. page 309 Edition: 2003 Published in Rabwah}

For any work, best results are achieved when work is done in a fresh state in the morning. This is not the case with people these days who stay up late or stay up all night either on the Internet or in front of TV or stay busy in other worldly affairs. They do not get enough sleep at night. They are still half asleep when they wake up in the morning. What kind of Salat can they offer? And what blessing will they get in other affairs? Everyone, including worldly individuals, makes effort to start fresh, to do their best work with full attention, so that the best results are achieved. Hence, the Promised Messiah (as) said that you should try to seek the best time for your prayers and when can you achieve the state that leads to acceptance of prayers".

- Friday Sermon delivered 15 March 2013 at Baitul Futuh Mosque, London
- Published AlFazl International 05 April 2013

In a Friday sermon, Huzoor-e-Anwar explained the importance of Fajr prayer and some hinderances in offering Fajr on time, and advised creating balance between worship and worldly affairs, as below:

"If parents wake up children for Fajr, they will learn the importance of Salat and they will be saved from frivolous activities. Those who are in the habit of staying up late to watch TV or browse the Internet, at least on the weekends when they have to wake up for Fajr, they will be forced to adopt the habit of going to bed early, and they will not waste their time. Especially those children, who are approaching adulthood, will develop a moderate approach to worldly activities. There are occasions when the use of such devices is needed, there are good things to view as well as information to be gained, I do not stop such use but I promote moderation. **It is extremely foolish to acquire these things at the risk of not offering Salat."**

After this, Huzoor-e-Anwar (aba) urged those living in western countries to offer prayers on time and to listen to the words of the Khalifa of the time and to act on them. He said:

"Again, I say that we need to analyze ourselves. People living in these countries do not pay attention to Salat due to worldly affairs. People living in urban areas of third world countries are also in a similar state. Nevertheless, there are some who still go to mosques. Just as the Khulafa before me, I have repeatedly drawn attention to this important Islamic obligation. In this age, Allah has granted MTA to us. Prior to this, the voice of Khalifa of the time could not reach every corner of the world instantaneously. Now his voice and the message of Allah and His Prophet (saw) reach every corner immediately. Those among us who do not listen to sermons or speeches or those that listen to them halfheartedly and do not pay attention to them are not fulfilling the pledge of initiation that 'I will give precedence to my faith over all worldly objects. I will completely obey you [Khalifatul Masih] in everything good that you may require of me.' Listening and ignoring [what the Khalifa says] leads to disobedience. These are actions that will take you away from obedience."

- Friday Sermon delivered 22 Jun 2012 at Baitur Rehman, Silver Spring, MD, USA
- Published AlFazl International 13 July 2012

Addressing the Khuddam at the Annual Ijtema in UK, Huzoor-e-Anwar especially instructed the young Ahmadi men to make Salat their primary objective. He said:

"Members of Khuddamul-Ahmadiyya are at an age and period in their lives where they have the most physical strength and also the greatest potential to progress and advance in all spheres of their lives. It should not be difficult for them to fulfill the obligations of the worship of Allah. And so all Khuddam and Atfal should be regular in their prayers and should offer them in congregation as much as possible. Every one of you should consider this to be a principle of paramount importance because it is through sincere worship that the gates to heaven are unlocked"

- Address at the Annual Ijtema Khuddam ul Ahmadiyya UK 26 September 2016, Kingsley, Surrey
- Published Weekly Badr Qadian 07 Sep 2017

A Believer Shuns all that is Vain

- Need to Raise the Standards of Modesty
- Vulgarity in the Name of Adornment
- International Spread of Societal Evils

A Believer Shuns all that is Vain

Need to Raise the Standards of Modesty

Irresponsible use of the latest inventions and modes of communications has resulted in extreme moral corruption in every society in this world. Huzoor-e-Anwar (aba) has repeatedly reminded members of the Jama'at and especially the youth to safeguard themselves against these societal evils. In this regard, he (aba) said the following in a Friday sermon:

"As I had mentioned earlier, the latest inventions such as TV and Internet have redefined the historically established standards of modesty. Even after showing blatant immodesty, they say it is not so. The standard of modesty of an Ahmadi is not how it is shown on TV and the Internet. This is not modesty: rather, it is people being embroiled in lust and passion. Immodesty and indecency have also changed the standards of modesty in some apparently decent Ahmadi household. In the name of progress, such [vulgar] things are discussed and such [vulgar] actions are taken, which are not permissible for any decent human, even if they are husband and wife. Some matters are such that when they are done in front of others, not only are they unwarrantable, they become a sin. If Ahmadi families do not clean their homes of such vulgarities, then they have not honored their pledge, which they had made at the hand of the Imam of this age, and they have wasted their belief.

The Holy Prophet (saw) clearly said:

$$ اَلْحَيَآءُ شُعْبَةٌ مِّنَ الْإِيْمَانِ $$

Modesty is part of faith. {Muslim Kitabul iman baab Shu'aib ul Iman wa Afzaluha Hadith number 59}

Hence, each Ahmadi youth should be especially cognizant of not getting ensnared by the transgressions shown by the Media; otherwise, they may lose their faith. Under the influence of these indecencies some individuals cross all limits and have to be excommunicate by way of punishment.

Always remember that all your actions should be done to please Allah.

A Hadith relates that Holy Prophet (saw) said: Indecency makes the perpetrator unsightly and modesty and bashfulness gives a modest person inner and outer beauty and makes him beautiful." {Tirmadhi Kitabul Birr wa Sila Bab maja'a fil Fuhsh wal Tafahhush. Hadith 1974}

- Friday Sermon delivered 15 January 2010 at Baitul Futuh Mosque, London
- Published AlFazl International 05 February 2010

Vulgarity in the Name of Adornment

On many occasions, Huzoor-e-Anwar (aba) has declared the trend of increasing immodesty in society to be extremely dangerous. He has often explained the Islamic teaching of Ghade-basr, meaning modestly lowering the gaze to safeguard oneself. In an address to the Ahmadi ladies he said:

"As I said, the attire is increasingly becoming an indecent attire. They advertise these [indecent clothes] through large billboards, advertisements on TV, advertisements on the Internet and even in newspapers. If a decent man happens to come across such advertisements, he lowers his gaze out of embarrassment, and he should lower his gaze. All this is done in the name of the modern society and broad mindedness. As I said, the clothing trends have become immodest. There is advertisement for indecency in the name of beauty."

- Address to the Ladies at Jalsa Salana Germany 29 June 2013 at Karlsruhe, Germany
- Published AlFazl International 18 October 2013

International Spread of Societal Evils

In the current age, the circle of transgression is expanding due to the extreme expansion of the communication system. Hence, drawing attention to the members of the community towards this important topic, Huzoor-e-Anwar (aba) said in a Friday sermon:

"These days the practical danger stems from the rampant and uncontrollable spread of the societal ills and, worse, some ills are given legal protection in the name of freedom of expression and speech. Evil was somewhat restricted before this age. The evil of the neighborhood remained in the neighborhood, a city's evil stayed in the city, and a country's evil remained in the country. At worst, neighbors would be affected by an evil. Now, however, with the ease of travel, television, Internet and various media these individual and localized evils have turned into international evils. Contacts are forged on the Internet across thousands of miles to spread evil and indecency."

- Friday Sermon delivered 06 Dec 2013 at Baitul Futuh Mosque, London
- Published AlFazl International 27 December 2013

****

Role of Parents in the Training of Children

- **Save your Future Generations from the Evils of Media**
- **Attend to the Training of Children from a Young Age**
- **Unnecessary use of Mobile Phones by Young Children**
- **Block Immoral Television Programs**

Role of Parents in the Training of Children

Save your Future Generations from the Evils of Media

On 23rd April 2010, our leader Huzoor-e-Anwar (aba) delivered an important Friday Sermon in Switzerland regarding the tarbiyyat (moral training) of the members of the Jama'at and especially the younger generations. He explained in detail different moral ills in various societies and especially the moral ills created in western societies by the latest technology. To deal with these, he drew the attention of the parents, Nizam-e-Jama'at (organization of Jama'at) and the auxiliary organizations. Huzoor-e-Anwar (aba) said:

"Sometimes one's children go against the word of God, which is a type of shirk [associating partners with Allah]. Disobeying a clear commandment of Allah the Exalted, so that one may agree with the demands of the children is a covert shirk. Such matters make one forget Allah the Exalted. Some people have distanced themselves from Ahmadiyyat because of their children. When excessive love for children and freedom given to children made the children leave the faith, the parents themselves left the faith. Allah, the Exalted states in the Holy Quran:

يَا أَيُّهَا الَّذِيْنَ اٰمَنُوْا لَا تُلْهِكُمْ أَمْوَالُكُمْ وَ لَا أَوْلَادُكُمْ عَنْ ذِكْرِ اللّٰهِ

'O ye who believe! let not your wealth and your children divert you from the remembrance of Allah...' [Holy Quran: 63:10]

"Then, the Promised Messiah (as) expects one to always safeguard oneself from falsehood, fornication, trespasses of the eye, quarrel, cruelty, dishonesty, mischief and rebellion. We need to constantly evaluate ourselves to see if we are staying away from these evils. Some people consider these things to be trivial and insignificant. They lie in their business and their affairs. They consider falsehood to be insignificant, even though Allah the Exalted has equated falsehood with shirk. The evils of fornication and trespasses of the eyes are common due to the media. In homes, through television or the Internet, such vulgar and obscene films and programs are shown that push a human toward evil. The young boys and girls in some Ahmadi homes have been engaged in such evils. In the beginning, such films are seen in the name of open-mindedness. Then some unfortunate homes get embroiled in these evils. **The fornication of the mind and the eyes is real and gradually this behavior leads to actual sin.** Parents [sometimes] are not careful in the beginning, but when the matter gets out of control, they lament and cry that our children have gone astray… our progeny has gone astray. Hence, it is important to be watchful. Do not let children sit in front of TV when vulgar programs are shown and be mindful of their Internet.

Some parents are not highly educated. It is the duty of the Nizam-e-Jama'at to make them aware. Similarly, Ansarullah, Lajna and Khuddam ul Ahmadiyya should make programs for their own auxiliaries to safeguard against these evils. Affiliate young boys and girls to the Nizam-e-Jama'at and the auxiliaries so that they always give precedence to their faith. **In this regard, mothers and fathers should fully cooperate with the Nizam-e-Jama'at or the auxiliary.** If the mother and father show weakness, then it will be tantamount to killing their children. **In particular, as the head of the household, men have the greatest duty and obligation to save their children from falling in the fire. Allah through His Benevolence, saved you or your elders from suffering the torment of the fire by enabling you or your elders to recognize the Imam of this age.** The world and especially other Muslims are anxious to find a leader who can guide them. You have been blessed by Allah that you receive guidance through the Bai'at of the Imam. By staying connected to the Khilafat, you are reminded of staying firm on virtues. Thus, the blessings of Allah demand that when reminded you should say Labbaik [Here I am] and make a pledge to avoid all evils. Establish virtues yourself and instruct your children to do the same and make efforts in this regard. Always remember this commandment and warning from Allah:

يَآَيُّهَا الَّذِيْنَ اٰمَنُوْا قُوٓا اَنْفُسَكُمْ وَ اَهْلِيْكُمْ نَارًا

'O ye who believe! save yourselves and your families from a Fire…' [Holy Quran 66:7]

These days the glitz and glamor of this world, vain vulgarities and many societal ills are standing in front of us trying to ensnare us and take us away from morality; though these are not considered ills by western standards, these are ills according to Islamic teachings. **As I said before, some wrong acts are done in the name of broad-mindedness, but then they keep pushing us towards evil. This is neither entertainment nor freedom; rather, these are pits of fire in the name of entertainment and freedom.** Allah the Exalted, who is extremely Gracious to His people, has clearly explained for the believers that this is fire. This is a fire; save yourself from it and save your children from it. I say to the young men and women who live in this society that this is not the objective of your lives. Do not think that the purpose of your life is to get involved in these vain pursuits; that this [lifestyle] is all there is for us. Through the status of being an Ahmadi, there should be a difference between you and others."

- Friday sermon delivered 23 April 2010 in Switzerland
- Published AlFazl International 14 May 2010

Attend to the Training of Children from a Young Age

In a Friday sermon Huzoor-e-Anwar (aba) explained how the environment affects the mind of children and plays a role in building their character. He said:

"In the fitrat (nature) of man, Allah the Exalted has placed a tendency to copy others in our surroundings, which manifests from childhood, as it is part of the nature of man. Hence, the tendency to copy others is in the nature of a child. This tendency is certainly for our benefit, but the wrong use sometimes leads to man's destruction or takes him towards destruction. It is a consequence of this tendency to copy and be influenced by his environment that man learns a language from one's parents, learns other deeds and good things which make a child a well-mannered person. If the parents are virtuous, observe the Salat, read and recite the Holy Quran, live with each other in an atmosphere of love and affection, and abhor falsehood, then the children under their influence will adopt virtues. On the contrary, if the child sees lying, fighting and disputes, making fun of others in the home, not giving due regard to the dignity of the Jama'at or other such bad actions, then because of that tendency to copy or because of the impact of the environment the child learns these evils. When he goes out, he tries to learn whatever he sees in his surroundings and among his friends. This is why I repeatedly draw attention to the parents that they should keep an eye on the outside environment of the children. And even within the home they should keep an eye on the programs that they watch on television or their Internet usage."

- Friday sermon delivered 13 December 2013 at Baitul Futuh Mosque, London
- Published AlFazl International 03 January 2014

Unnecessary use of Mobile phones by Young Children

Huzoor (aba) has warned us about the negative influence of the wrong use of the latest technology including mobile phones on the character of children. Advising young Ahmadi men and children at the occasion of the Ijtema of Atfal ul Ahamdiyya Germany, he (aba) said:

"There is a widespread problem here of children demanding from their parents to buy them mobile phones. Some are just 10 years of age and say that they should have a mobile phone. Are you doing some sort of business? Or are you are doing some kind of work in which information is required to be accessed every minute? When asked, they reply 'we need to call our parents.' If your parents are not worried, there is also no need for you to worry, because phones can also lead to bad habits. Through phones, some people contact children directly and then incite them into bad habits. Hence, the phone is also a very harmful thing due to which children lose all good sense and get involved in wrongdoings, so avoid this. As for the TV programs, as I said you may watch cartoons or informative programs. However, you must avoid all vulgar and indecent programs."

- Address at National Itfal tul Ahmadiyya Ijtema Germany 16 September 2011
- Published AlFazl Internatonl 09 March 2012

Block Immoral Television Programs

For the sake of entertainment, not only children, but even adults sit for hours in front of the television. As a result of this, some people lose the ability to discern what is evil. Hence, Huzoor-e-Anwar (aba) advised against watching immoral television programs and treading the dangerous path of indecency. He said:

"Hence, an utmost effort is needed to safeguard oneself from the Satanic attacks. In this regard, Allah the Exalted says that 'Ahsan Qaul' [good word] is needed."

In this regard, Huzoor-e-Anwar explained the Quranic commandment of 'Qaul-e-Sadid' [the true word] mentioned in Sura Al-Furqan verse 70. He (aba) said:

"To attain standards of truthfulness, it is further enjoined to promptly leave gatherings where there is no truthfulness and where crude and vain talk take place. Do not go to gatherings where there is talk against the teachings of Allah the Exalted. Sometimes, in family gatherings or our own gatherings, unconsciously things are said which are vain and crude: things are said against the Nizam (administrative system). I have mentioned it many times before that if there are issues regarding the office holders and reformation is not taking place at lower levels, then these should be brought to my attention. However, if you talk about these things in gatherings, they become vain talk because [carelessly talking about them] does not lead to reformation. On the contrary, it will lead to further discord, conflicts, and disputes.

Then, in this age, there are obscene films on TV. There are extremely vulgar and indecent films on the Internet. There are dances and songs. Some Indian film songs depict praying to gods and goddesses or they are being extolled which negates the power of One Powerful God. Or these gods, goddesses and idols are professed as the source of nearness to God. This is vain and is Shirk (associating partners with God). Shirk equates falsehood. [We] must not listen to such songs."

Huzoor-e-Anwar (aba) also said:

"Allah says:

وَإِمَّا يَنْزَغَنَّكَ مِنَ الشَّيْطٰنِ نَزْغٌ فَاسْتَعِذْ بِاللّٰهِ ۚ إِنَّهُ سَمِيْعٌ عَلِيْمٌ ۰

'And if an evil suggestion from Satan incite thee, then seek refuge in Allah; surely, He is All-Hearing, All-Knowing.' [Holy Quran 7:201]

If Satan says something to incite you or he brings to you such conversation that are against the "Ahsan Qaul" [good word], then seek refuge with Allah. You should pray a lot to come under Allah's protection. We should say the prayer:

$$\text{أَعُوْذُ بِاللّٰهِ مَنِ الشَّيْطٰنِ الرَّجِيْمِ} \circ$$

'I seek refuge with Allah against Satan the accursed'

Say:

$$\text{لَا حَوْلَ وَلَا قُوَّةَ إِلَّا بِاللّٰه}$$

'There is no might nor power except through Allah'
Allah, Who sees and listens, gives us hope that if a prayer is made with sincerity of intent, God certainly listens."

- Friday sermon delivered 18 October 2013 at Baitul Huda Mosque, Sydney, Australia
- Published AlFazl International 08 November 2013

On several occasions Huzoor-e-Anwar has advised us to avoid vain things (which include TV and the Internet). At the occasion of Lajna Ima'illah Ijtema in Germany, he (aba) said:

"Then there is idle and vain talk. I especially need to draw the attention of young children towards the fact that idle talk is not merely conversations carried on by elderly women, who do it and should abstain from it. However, TV and Internet are now considered vain for the girls between the ages of 10 to 12 years old and young ladies, as well. If you are spending your entire day watching programs which contain no moral lesson, then this amounts to a vain and useless activity. Furthermore, on the Internet, you sometimes visit such sites from where there is no point of return and this continuously spreads immorality. Sometimes such cases are reported in which girls are trapped by boys in wrong groups and have to leave their homes; thus, becoming a disgrace for their families and the Jama'at. Therefore, it is extremely important to save yourself from the Internet etc. Other than this, there are many other programs on the Internet that poison minds. There are many immoral programs on TV. Parents should block such channels, which leave a filthy effect on the mind of children. Such channels should be kept on a permanent block. When children watch TV for 1 to 2 hours, however much they want to watch they can do so, but they should only watch decent and wholesome dramas and cartoons. If they are watching something indecent, it is the responsibility of the parent. And 12 or 13-year-old girls who are in an age of consciousness, it is their responsibility to stay away from such programs. You are an Ahmadi and the character of an Ahmadi should be distinct and unique from others. It should be clear that this is an Ahmadi girl."

- Address delivered at Annual Ijtema Lajna Ima'illah Germany 17 September 2011
- Published AlFazl International 16 November 2012

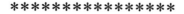

An Extremely Important Message from Hazrat Khalifatul Masih V (aba)

"I repeatedly draw attention of the parents that they should keep an eye on the outside environment of the children. And even within the home, they should keep an eye on the programs that they watch on the television or their Internet usage."

(Friday Sermon delivered 13 December 2013 at Baitul Futuh Mosque, London)

Responsibility of Mothers in the Current Age

رَبَّنَا هَبْ لَنَا مِنْ أَزْوَاجِنَا وَ ذُرِّيَّتِنَا قُرَّةَ أَعْيُنٍ
وَّ اجْعَلْنَا لِلْمُتَّقِينَ إِمَامًا ه

"Our Lord, grant us of our wives and children the delight
of our eyes, and make us a model for the righteous."
(Holy Quran 25:75).

Responsibility of Mothers in the Current Age

In this address, Huzoor-e-Anwar explained to the members of Lajna Ima'illah the signs of the Ibad-ur-Rahman (Men of Gracious God) and advised them to avoid all that is vain. He said:

"Allah the Almighty also says, that a believer abstains from frivolity. This is another sign that instead of pursuing frivolous pursuits, you should maintain your dignity with the thought that as an Ahmadi it is not your job to indulge in useless worldly trivialities. Just move forward while refraining from them. For instance, nowadays there are various television channels, which air extremely vulgar and profane programs. At times some decent programs are also being aired, but during these some extremely vulgar and obscene advertisements are shown. Hence, it is the responsibility of every Ahmadi, be it a child, a young girl, boy, woman or man, that when such programs are aired, even if an inappropriate image is aired, they should turn them off. As I mentioned, even if such advertisements are aired, they should not be viewed. An Ahmadi should completely abstain from such vulgar programs.

There are certain websites on the Internet which show extremely obscene programs. It is the sign of a true believer to protect himself from it. Refrain from these vulgarities and profanities. It is absolutely essential to do so in order to seek Allah the Almighty's reward and blessings.

Allah the Almighty has called upon us to pray. It is a sign of such people who pray:

رَبَّنَا هَبْ لَنَا مِنْ أَزْوَاجِنَا وَ ذُرِّيّٰتِنَا قُرَّةَ أَعْيُنٍ وَّ اجْعَلْنَا لِلْمُتَّقِيْنَ إِمَامًا o

'Our Lord, grant us of our wives and children the delight of our eyes, and make us a model for the righteous." (Holy Quran 25:75).

This prayer will not only keep you steadfast on the path of righteousness, but will also safeguard your progeny from the evils of this world and guide them towards righteousness. This prayer will also be in favor of those women who complain that their husbands do not maintain an affiliation with the faith and are irregular in the daily prayers. Allah will indeed listen to the prayers generated from the depts of our heart. Do not think that only men are the leaders of the righteous people. **Every woman who prays for her child and tries to inculcate in her future generations the spirit of bonding with Allah, [encourages] the act of prostrating before Him and [encourages] remaining steadfast on the path of righteousness will endeavor to be the leader of the righteous ones. As a caretaker of her house, she is an Imam [leader]."**

- Address at Lajna Ima'illah Annual Ijtema 04 November 2007 UK at Baitul Futuh Mosque, London
- Published AlFazl International 09 December 2016

In regards to the responsibility of the mothers, Huzoor-e-Anwar (aba) instructed members of the National Majlis-e-Amila Ireland:

"There is nothing wrong with getting an education [at an institution] where boys and girls are being schooled together; as long as boys are not befriending the girls and they talk to each other only as needed. They should avoid [communication through] SMS, Facebook, online chat and phone calls. Instruct the parents to keep an eye on children. It is not right to always have a computer or mobile phone in hand. **Mothers who don't**

know how to work with computers should learn in order to keep an eye on [their] children."

- National Majlise Amila Lajna Imaillah Meeting Ireland 18 September 2010
- Published AlFazl International 22 October 2010

Similarly, Huzoor-e-Anwar has instructed Ahmadi women to safeguard their homes from the influence of social frivolities and absurdities:

"In the same way, vain things also include obscene and vulgar movies, books [and] magazines. These are spread in the market under the excuse that sexual relations should become known in this day and age, so one can safeguard against ills. It is uncertain whether they save anyone, but the morally depraved advertisements of this type that are visible on each street and street corner do indeed embroil society in sin. A thing that is natural will become apparent on its own at the time when there is a need to know about it. One should safeguard oneself from this immoral mental indulgence in the name of knowledge. **This is why the Promised Messiah (as) has said, 'safeguard every part of your body from fornication.'** Thus, every woman should talk to her children about this with a certain concern. And every girl who has reached puberty, whose mind has matured, should have the awareness that these evils will keep pushing one further and further into filth, and so one must safeguard against them.

Anything which is wrongfully used is considered vain. For instance, I have mentioned the Internet several times before. It is an invention of this age and Allah the Exalted had destined these inventions for the age of the Promised Messiah (as). [God Almighty] has alluded to various inventions in the Holy Qur'an; the Internet is one of them; the current telephone system is one of them; the television system is also one of them. These are to be used for propagation [of faith] in this age. But if these inventions are used for the wrong reason, then they are considered vain and God has forbidden such vain things. God has also commanded to safeguard against them.

He says that the description of a true believer ['momin'] is that:

$$ \text{عَنِ اللَّغْوِ مُعْرِضُوْنَ} \circ $$

They "…shun all that which is vain…" (Holy Quran, 23: 4)

[That is,] they safeguard against that which is vain. When you use the Internet to chat with friends, make fun of others, use lewd language, use it against each other, use it to cause rifts in people's relationships, [use it to] ruin another woman's life by talking to her husband on the Internet, or [where you] backbite against each other, then the same useful object becomes vain and will also become a sin. These days, text messages are sent using mobile phones. This is another practice that has started these days. It offers a very inexpensive way to waste time in frivolities and talking with those who are not mehrum ['non-marriageable relatives according to Islam']. Very casually it is said that, 'it was only a text message, it's not like we were talking.' Contacts are developed with others when a girl's female friend gives the phone number of a [male] friend of hers, or [contact] numbers are exchanged in some other way, and text messages start getting exchanged over the phone. Girls and boys -- 12, 13, 14 years old -- are walking around [with cell phones] sending messages. They are at an age where they are at risk of going astray and eventually, this leads to sins developing from these vain [pursuits]. And this is why Ahmadi girls, for the sake of their honor, for the sake of their dignity, for the sake of their family's honor, [and] keeping in mind the sanctity of their Jama'at with which they are thought to be affiliated, they should stay away from these things. And likewise, the Ahmadi men listening to this, should also safeguard themselves against this."

- Address at Annual Ijtema Lajna Ima'illah Germany 11 June 2006
- Published AlFazl International 19 June 2015

****

Exhortations to Ahmadi Girls

- Chatting on Social Media and Immodesty through Pictures of Women
- Purdah-Saves One from Overt and Covert Fahsha (foul deeds)
- Caution in using Facebook
- Girls should do Tabligh only to Girls
- Marriages outside the Community and their Tragic Results due to the Wrong use of Internet and Social Media

Exhortations to Ahmadi Girls

To reap the blessings of Ahmadiyyat, it is essential to adopt the restrictions required by Islam and obey the commandments of Allah the Exalted. In this regard, Huzoor-e-Anwar (aba) said:

"Sometimes, after reaching a certain age some young girls feel that religion may be imposing certain restrictions on them. I have said do not watch certain television channels and websites that are obscene and frivolous. At times, under the influence of others, questions are raised as to what is the harm in watching these and that 'we do not repeat the acts that are shown on TV channels.' Always remember that after watching these two, four or six times, the same actions start manifesting. **Some households were destroyed merely as a result of asking, 'what difference does it make?' Those households lost not only religion, but worldly benefits and their children as well. Thus, the question of, 'what difference would it make? There should be some freedom' is extremely detrimental.** When Allah the Almighty tells us to protect ourselves from 'all that is vain'; it is because He is well aware of the nature of His creation. He knows all that can occur in the name of freedom. Always remember that Satan openly challenged Allah the Almighty that he would come to lure all beings who are the descendants of Adam in every possible way, except those who are Ibaad urRahman [the servants of the Gracious Lord].

Thus, the misuse of some current technological inventions is one of the satanic attacks. Hence, every Ahmadi girl should endeavor to protect herself from it. Always think that you are an Ahmadi and in order to remain an Ahmadi, you should refrain from these profanities. Always remember that we have believed in the truthfulness of Ahmadiyyat, considered the Promised Messiah (as) to be truthful and have entered his Bai'at, considering him to be the absolute truth. Hence, we should try to refrain from all such things which Allah the Almighty has prohibited. Only then will we be able to partake of the blessings promised by Almighty Allah to the Promised Messiah (as)."

- Address at the Annual Ijtema Lajna Ima'illah UK 04 November 2007 at Baitul Futuh Mosque, London
- Published AlFazl International 09 December 2016

Chatting on Social Media and Immodesty through Pictures of Women

Increasing mutual connection and exchange of pictures of females is against our moral values and should be absolutely avoided by Ahmadi youth, girls and children. Huzoor-e-Anwar (aba) warned regarding this important issue:

"These days a new method of introduction has been created on the computer and the Internet called Facebook. Though it is not that new, but it was introduced in the last few years. I had previously discouraged you from this practice. I had said in my sermons that it encourages immodesty. It shatters the boundaries among people, boundaries from one another, boundaries around secrets. It exposes secrets and invites indecency. The creator of this site has said, 'I have created this and I believe that whatever a man is on the outside and inside should be exposed to others.' In his view, exposing someone means that if someone wants to post a nude picture of himself, he may and even encourages others to comment on it. This is allowed! Innalillah ["To Allah we return"]. Similarly, anyone can post about anything he sees. If this is not extreme moral regression and degradation, then what is? In this state of moral regression and degradation, an Ahmadi has to teach the high standard of morality and virtue."

- Concluding Address Jalsa Salana Germany 26 June 2011

Similarly, Huzoor-e-Anwar (aba) instructed mothers to provide alternative activities to young girls to safeguard them from the ill effects of Social Media. He said:

"These days many ills are developing through Social Media. Young boys and girls, sitting in front of their parents, are silently chatting where pictures and messages are being exchanged. New accounts are being created in new programs and the entire day is wasted on the phone, iPad or computer etc. This leads to worsening of morals and gives rise to irritability in character and the children quickly become out of control. All these matters need attention and there is need to impose limits. For this, you will need to think about creating alternative means of occupying their time. Keep them involved in house work. Involve them in serving the Jama'at and develop means of occupying them that are positive and beneficial to the society. This is a very important responsibility that Ahmadi ladies have to fulfill."

• Message for Annual Ijtema Lajna Ima'illah Germany 10 July 2016

Purdah-saves one from overt and covert Fahsha (foul deeds)

In a Friday sermon, Huzoor-e-Anwar (aba) warned members of the Jama'at of the horrible outcome of the spread of indecency through various means. He explained in detail, the Islamic teaching in this regard, referencing verses 152 and 153 of Sura Al Anam. Huzoor-e-Anwar (aba) said:

"Allah the Exalted says do not approach foul deeds. This means to stay away from all those things that incite one towards foul deeds. In this age, many different means [of foulness] have been created. There is the Internet which has lewd films on the websites; TV also has vulgar films. There are vulgar and indecent magazines. Voices are being raised against indecent pornographic magazines that such magazine should not be displayed openly in shops and stalls as it has an adverse effect on children's morality. They have realized this today, while the Holy Qur'an gave the teaching 1400 years ago to stay away from indecency. The indecency makes one immoral, distant from God and religion, and even makes one break the law. Islam does not only forbid obvious and apparent foulness, but also hidden immorality. The directive of purdah is such so that purdah and wearing modest clothes create a safeguard against open and informal connections between men and women.

Islam does not state as the Bible does that do not look at women with bad intent. In fact, it states that seeing a woman will create affection which will create immodesty and you will not be able to distinguish between good and bad. According to Allah and His Messenger (saw), when a boy and a girl, a man and a woman openly meet with each other, then the third among them is Satan. {Sunan AtTirmazi Kitab urriza bab ma ja fi kiraheyaatil dakhool alal mugheebat hadith number 117}

I have given you the example of the Internet. Chatting on Facebook and Skype are included in this. I have seen many families break up because of this. I have to say with great regret that such incidents are found even in our Ahmadi homes. We should always remember the commandment of Allah not to even come near foulness; otherwise, Satan will overtake us.

The beautiful teaching of the Holy Qur'an does not just forbid women from looking [at the other gender] or avoiding eye contact, rather it commands both men and women to lower their gaze. A lowered gaze precludes open mixing [of men and women] and watching lewd films. The commandment also says not to socialize with people who pursue such interests in the name of freedom, who relate their stories and try to incite others to their ways. **Men and women should not chat on Skype and Facebook and look at each other and should not make these a means of connecting with each other. God states that these** are all open and hidden foul things and they result in one getting carried away with emotions, losing one's sense and judgement and eventually incurring God's displeasure by disobeying His commandment."

- Friday Sermon delivered 02 August 2013 at Baitul Futuh Mosque, London
- Published AlFazl International 23 August 2013

Caution in using Facebook

Answering a question regarding Facebook from a girl during a Waaqifat-e-Nau girls' class, Huzoor (aba) said:

"I did not say that if you do not give it up, you will become a sinner. Instead, I said that it has more harms and very few benefits. These days, those boys and girls who have a Facebook page, reach a place where immorality begins to spread. Boys try to make connections. In certain cases, girls are trapped into posting their unveiled pictures on Facebook. At home, under normal circumstances, you share your picture with a girlfriend, she further posts it on her Facebook, and gradually it spreads from Hamburg to New York (America) and reaches Australia, and from there connections are initiated. Then, groups are formed of men and of women and the pictures are altered, which may be used for blackmailing. Therefore, it is safer not to go there at all."

Huzoor-e-Anwar (aba) also said:

"My task is to advise. The Holy Quran says to keep on admonishing. Those who do not pay heed, their sins are their own burden. If Tabligh (propagation) is to be done on Facebook, then do tabligh through it. It is present on Al Islam website; it is used for tabligh there."

Huzoor-e-Anwar said:

"Girls are easily fooled. Whoever showers praise on you, you will say no one is better, but if parents offer genuine advice, you say we have been educated in Germany while you have arrived from some village."

Huzoor-e-Anwar mentioned a hadith and said:

اَلْحِكْمَةُ ضَالَّةُ الْمُؤْمِن

"Wisdom is the lost property of a believer"
"This means you should take up a good thing wherever you find it. All their inventions are not beneficial. Those girls who do not heed my advice, later write to me crying, that they stumbled, and have been trapped in such a situation... The person who created Facebook himself admitted that 'I designed it so I can expose everyone to the world.' Does an Ahmadi girl want to be exposed? Those who do not listen, it is up to them."

- Waqifat-e-Nau Class Germany 08 October 2011 at Baitur Rasheed Mosque
- Published AlFazl International 06 January 2012

Girls should do Tabligh only to girls

Huzoor-e-Anwar (aba) has repeatedly advised us that Ahmadi girls should only do tabligh to girls. In this regard, he advised the office holders of Lajna Ima'illah and said:

"Lajna Tabligh department should make teams of women and girls and use them for tabligh. **However, it should be clearly remembered that girls should only do tabligh to other females.** Some people make tabligh contacts on the Internet. Tabligh contacts on the Internet should only be established with women and girls. Leave tabligh towards men for the men, because [otherwise] this causes some issues. It is said that we are doing tabligh; however, what has generally been seen and experienced is that these Internet connections lead to some results that are not appropriate for an Ahmadi female. Girls who are studying in college and universities should talk to other female students about themselves and Islam without any hesitation, embarrassment or inferiority complex. Tell them who we are and, in this way, introduce them to Islam."

- Address to Ladies Jalsa Salana Australia 15 April 2006
- Published AlFazl International 12 June 2015

Many girls use Internet for the purpose of tabligh (preaching) and think that this is safer and more effective as compared to direct tabligh. However, soon thereafter, negative consequences manifest themselves. Therefore, Huzoor (aba) gave an important advice about applying Islamic teachings on purdah to current technology. Huzoor-e-Anwar (aba) said:

"Now I would like to say something pertaining to chatting on the Internet, which also comes under the category of non-observance of purdah. Casually, you connect online and start chatting without realizing with whom you are talking to. Our girls are chatting without knowing whether it is a girl or a boy sitting at the other end. Sometimes boys hide their identity and pretend to be girls to talk to girls.

It has been brought to my attention that our girls talk to boys considering them to be girls and start introducing the Jama'at to them. Our girl, in her mind, is happy that she is calling them towards Allah. She does not know the intentions of [the boy posing to be] the other girl. Even if you have a good intention, you don't know the intentions of the boy sitting at the other end. How would you know? Gradually, it goes to the level where pictures are exchanged. Now, showing your pictures is the extreme of immodesty. In some situations, it has even ended up in a marriage. As I mentioned that it has led to frightening results. Most of these marriages failed within a short while.

Remember, if you would like to preach, then girls should only preach to girls. Girls don't have to preach to boys. Leave it to the boys to do that. As I mentioned earlier, this is a societal ill and we are facing very frightening results."

- Address at Annual Ijtema Lajna Ima'illah UK 19 October 2003 Baitul Futuh Mosque, London
- Published AlFazl International 17 April 2015

Marriages outside the community and their tragic results due to wrong use of the Internet and Social Media

A few Ahmadi girls and ladies married non-Ahmadi men resulting from relationships that started on the Internet. However, within a short time frame such marriages failed and resulted in dangerous consequences of taking future generations away from Ahmadiyyat. Huzoor-e-Anwar warned Ahmadi ladies in this regard and said:

"Today, there is the Internet. In the past, wherever a woman married a man who did not belong to the Jama'at, later wrote expressing regret and embarrassment that it was a mistake to marry men outside the Jama'at. Boys are more attached to the father and in particular to a non-Ahmadi father as they grant more freedom. Even if the girls maintain some connection with the Jama'at under the influence of the mother, the father insists on marrying them outside the Jama'at. Some girls raise their voice against their fathers. Some write that they should be helped as they do not want to marry outside the Jama'at. Others are forced into it. Thus, mothers and fathers should pay attention that there should be no contact established through the Internet. You should explain to them in a calm and loving manner. Those girls who have reached an age of maturity should understand the matter. Otherwise they should remember that they would be giving children, from the womb of Ahmadi mothers, to those outside the community. Why are you committing this injustice against yourself and your future generations?"

- Address at Annual Ijtema Lajna Ima'illah UK 19 October 2003 Baitul Futuh Mosque, London
- Published AlFazl International 17 April 2015

****

"**Lajna Tabligh department should make teams of women and girls and use them for tabligh. However, it should be clearly remembered that girls should only do tabligh to other females...**"

(An extract from Annual Ijtema Lajna Ima'illah UK 19 October 2003 by Hazrat Khalifatul Masih V (aba))

Guidance for the Youth

- **Exhortation to the Youth to Act according to Islamic Teachings**
- **Ghade basr (Lowering of gaze): Jihad of Nafs (Self)**
- **Habit Hinders the Effort of Reformation**
- **Comprehensive Prayers to Avoid Evil**

Guidance for the Youth

Exhortation to the youth to act according to Islamic teachings

Huzoor-e-Anwar (aba) has repeatedly reminded the Ahmadi youth and children to live life according the traditions of the Jama'at and keeping the pledge in mind. In a special message for the Annual Ijtema of Majlis Khuddam ul Ahmadiyya India, Huzoor (aba) said:

"In your Ijtemaat and meetings, you repeat the pledge that you will give precedence to faith over all worldly matters. To achieve this, each one of you should regularly recite the Holy Quran, for it is a spiritual light which really teaches us how we can give precedence to our faith over all worldly matters. The Holy Quran teaches us that true believers offer Salat with due regard. Hence, each one of you should make five daily Salat the objective of your lives and, as much as possible, offer Salat in congregation because there is a greater reward in congregational Salat. Congregational Salat becomes a source of unity and cohesiveness and reflects the unity and might of a community of believers. Your Ijtemaat should be such that you compete with each other in piety and righteousness. Young Khuddam and older Atfal should stay in the company of good friends and good people. Misuse of the Internet and Social Media is becoming common. If a thing or an act leads to harmful effects on the mind, then it is considered 'lughv' (a vain thing) **and a characteristic of believers is that they avoid all that is vain.**

Similarly, it is also obligatory on men to safeguard their piety and modesty. They have been commanded to observe ghade basr (lowering of gaze) and should keep their gaze lowered and hearts and mind safeguarded against impure thoughts and bad intentions. Each Islamic principle is based on wisdom and strong reasoning. Through ghade basr, Islam teaches control of the self. Thus, you should remember that piety is an important characteristic trait of a Khadim which can lead one to attain spiritual heights. "

- Message for Annual Ijtema Khuddam and Atfal ul Ahmadiyya, India 10 October 2017
- Published Weekly Badr Qadian 02 November 2017

Huzoor-e-Anwar (aba) gave comprehensive instructions to Khuddam about developing noble character and self-control. He said:

"Further there are many other vices and ills that are spreading immorality in today's society and sadly they are increasing by the day. For example, the misuse of the Internet and Social Media is becoming increasingly common and this includes inappropriate chatting between boys and girls online. Similarly, the Internet is being used to watch indecent and immoral films including pornography. The smoking of cigarettes or the use of shisha are also examples of vices that are spreading. Furthermore, even the permissible things can cause harm if they are misused. One example of this is where a person stays awake late into the night watching television or surfing the Internet and then fails to wake up for the Fajr prayer, even if what they were viewing was not bad in itself. The end result is that they are moving away from righteousness and in this way the permissible act becomes immoral and not in keeping with the status of a true Muslim. In essence anything at all that has poisonous or detrimental effect on a person's mind is included in what the Holy Quran has deemed as vain."

Referring to verse 6 of Sura Al Mominoon, Huzoor-e-Anwar (aba) said:

"Allah the Almighty has stipulated another sign of a believer.

Allah the Almighty states:

وَ الَّذِيْنَ هُمْ لِفُرُوْجِهِمْ حٰفِظُوْنَ ٥

And who guard their chastity [Holy Quran 23:6]

To safeguard and protect one's chastity and modesty is certainly not only the task of women but is also incumbent upon men. To guard one's chastity does not only mean that the person should avoid sexual relations outside of marriage, rather the Promised Messiah (as) has taught us that it means that a believer should always keep his eyes and ears pure from anything that is indecent or immoral. As I mentioned earlier one thing that is completely obscene is pornography and to view it is to forgo the chastity of one's eyes and ears. It is also wrong and against Islamic teachings of modesty for boys and girls to mix freely, to form relationships or inappropriate friendships."

- Address to Khudam at Annual Ijtema UK 26 September 2016 Kingsley, Surrey
- Published Weekly Badr Qadian 07 September 2017

Ghade basr (Lowering of gaze): Jihad of Nafs (Self)

The current age is of the Jihad of the self rather than the Jihad of the sword. One can only stay on the path of piety by following the teachings of the Holy Quran. In this regard, explaining the importance of controlling human emotions and ghade basr (lowering of gaze), Huzoor-e-Anwar (aba) said in a Friday sermon:

"We Ahmadis should remember that the world is going through a dangerous time. Satan is aggressively striking from all directions and if Muslims and specially Ahmadi Muslim men, women, and youth do not try to uphold the religious values, then there is no guarantee of our future. We will be held accountable by God the Almighty more than others because we understood the truth that the Promised Messiah (as) explained to us yet we did not act upon it. Thus, if we want to save ourselves from destruction then it is imperative to live in this world while adopting every Islamic teaching with full confidence. Don't think that the progress of the advanced countries is a guarantee of our progress and life and walking with them will guarantee our survival. The progress of these advanced countries has reached its peak and their immorality and immoral actions are causing them to decline, which has begun manifesting itself. They are inviting the wrath of God, they are inviting destruction. Thus, in such a situation under human compassion, we have to show them the right path and save them, instead of adopting their colors. Their reformation seems to be difficult due to their arrogance and distance from religion. If they do not reform themselves then the future progress of the world will be led by those nations who keep the religious and moral values intact.

Thus, as I said before, I am especially addressing the youth that they should pay attention to God Almighty's teachings. Instead of getting influenced by the world and walking behind them, you should make the world follow you."

Huzoor-e-Anwar (aba) further stated:

"For the progress of Islam, all that is commanded by God and His messenger Prophet Muhammad (saw) is essential. The restrictions for modesty are not only for women. In Islam, restrictions are equal for both men and women. God Almighty first taught the way of modesty and purdah to men. He says:

قُلْ لِّلْمُؤْمِنِيْنَ يَغُضُّوْا مِنْ اَبْصَارِهِمْ وَ يَحْفَظُوْا فُرُوْجَهُمْ ذٰلِكَ اَزْكٰى لَهُمْ اِنَّ اللّٰهَ خَبِيْرٌ بِمَا يَصْنَعُوْنَ o

"Say to the believing men that they restrain their eyes and guard their private parts. That is purer for them. Surely, Allah is well aware of what they do." [Holy Quran 24:31]

God Almighty first commanded faithful men to do ghade basr (lowering of gaze) because it is necessary for purity. If there is no purity, then one cannot find God. Thus, before commanding women to do purdah, men are commanded to refrain from all that which may incite their emotions. They are prohibited from seeing women with open eyes, mixing with women, watching vulgar films, and chatting with Namehram people on Facebook or through Social Media; all these do not maintain chastity. That is why Promised Messiah (as) very clearly spoke about it on several occasions. He said,

"It is the Word of God alone that, by its very clear and open statements, lays down specific and well-defined limits and parameters for all our words and deeds, action and inaction, and teaches us the norms of humanity and the way of purity; it alone emphatically stresses upon the safeguarding of one's organs— like the eyes, ears, tongue, etc.— as He says:

$$\text{قُلْ لِّلْمُؤْمِنِيْنَ يَغُضُّوْا مِنْ اَبْصَارِهِمْ وَ يَحْفَظُوْا فُرُوْجَهُمْ}$$

$$\text{ذٰلِكَ اَزْكٰى لَهُمْ}$$

'Say to the believing men that they restrain their eyes and guard their private parts. That is purer for them." [Holy Quran 24:31].

This means that the believers should guard their eyes and ears, and private parts from those who are not mahram and should refrain from seeing, hearing, and doing all that is forbidden. Thus would they be able to foster inner purity. That is to say, their hearts will be safeguarded from diverse types of passions, for these are the organs which primarily incite the carnal passions and provoke beastly traits. Observe, therefore, how the Holy Quran stresses safeguarding oneself from those who are not mahram and how explicitly it urges believers to restrain their eyes, ears, and private parts to avoid any occasion that might lead to impurity." [Baraheen-e-Ahmadiyya vol 3 Rohani Khazain vol 1 page 209 margin)

- Friday Sermon Delivered 13 January 2017 at Baitul Futuh Mosque, London
- Published AlFazl International 03 February 2017

Habit hinders the effort of reformation

Established habits create hindrance in taking practical steps towards reformation. Regarding this important matter, Huzoor-e-Anwar (aba) said:

"A man was in the habit of swearing all the time and during every conversation. Often, he would not even realize that he was swearing. When a complaint was sent to Hazrat Musleh Maud (radi-Allahu'anhu [ra] May Allah be pleased with him), he sent for the person and asked him why he swore often? The person swore and asked who says I swear? Thus, once a habit is established, one does not realize what one is saying. Habits lead one to a state where one loses all awareness of it and all awareness is erased. However, if a person makes an effort then he can create awareness and work to reform [these habits].

Hence, habits create a strong impediment against practical acts [of reformation]. These days, people are drawn to watching unsuitable films. **People are interested in the films as if they were addicted to them. They do not eat, but simply sit and continue watching films. If they sit on the Internet, they will continue sitting there.** Even if they are falling asleep, they just continue sitting there, not caring about their wife and children. Such people exist. Thus, these habits play a major role in obstructing practical reformation."

Huzoor-e-Anwar (aba) further said:

"I will present an example for women, which is the state of purdah and modesty. Once it is removed things can go very far. While in Australia, I came to know that some elderly ladies, who had recently arrived from Pakistan to live with their families in Australia, advised their younger non-purdah observing family members to observe purdah and at least wear modest clothes and take headscarf. The girls who do not observe purdah told these elderly ladies that observing purdah was a crime in Australia and they too should give it up. Afraid of committing crimes, these ladies who had observed purdah all their lives gave it up, even though there is no such law, or restriction in Australia about purdah. No one pays attention to it. Some young girls and ladies have given up purdah for the sake of fashion. A young woman from Pakistan who has come to Australia after getting married wrote to me that she was forcibly asked to give up purdah or was influenced by the surroundings and had given it up. However, she wrote that when she listened to my address to the ladies about purdah during Jalsa, she had her burqa on and she has kept it on and is trying and praying to continue to do so and requested prayers. Purdah is being abandoned because the Quranic commandment is not reminded often enough and it is not spoken about in families. Thus, it is very important for reformation of practice to continually mention what is evil and what is virtuous."

- Friday Sermon Delivered 20 December 2013 at Baitul Futuh Mosque, London
- Published AlFazl International 10 January 2014

Comprehensive prayers to avoid evil

Inappropriate use of the latest technology and media in the current age is indeed a Satanic act. Prayers have become even more important to safeguard against the Satanic attacks. In this regard, advising the members of the Jama'at, Huzoor (aba) said:

"The Holy Prophet (saw) (May peace and blesings of Allah be upon him) was so concerned about saving the believers from the attack of Satan, that he (saw) taught his companions prayers to save them from Satan, and he taught them comprehensive prayers. A companion narrated that he (saw) taught us this prayer:

"O Allah create love in our hearts, reform us, and make us tread upon the paths of security, and take us to light saving us from darkness, and save us from overt and covert indecencies, and place blessings for us in our ears, in our eyes, in our hearts, in our wives and in our children, and turn to us with mercy. You are the acceptor of repentance and the one who forgives time and again. Make us the ones who are grateful for your favors and appreciate them and accept them. And, O Allah, perfect Your favors on us." {Sunan Abu Daud Kitabus Salat Bab Al- Tashahud hadith 969}

Thus, this is the prayer to restrain from inappropriate worldly entertainment and to save from all other kinds of useless things and to save from the attacks of Satan.

Even today, various improprieties are taking place in the world in the name of entertainment. When a man prays for blessings for the ears and the eyes, prays for peace and for moving from darkness to light, and prays for the ability to discharge the rights of wives and for children to be the delight of eyes, then his attention will automatically be diverted from improprieties and immoralities. This way a believer will become a source of saving the whole house from Satan."

- Friday Sermon delivered 20 May 2016 Gottenburg, Sweden
- Published AlFazl International 10 June 2016

Every human has a duty to give up the dark ways of Satan and to come to those lighted paths that lead to salvation. Explaining this subject, Huzoor-e-Anwar (aba) said in a Friday sermon:

"If one tries to reform himself in this manner, then it becomes a path to salvation for him. A man should look for ways to salvation for his own sake. Otherwise, he is told that he will move from light into darkness. This is the way to Satan which takes one from light into darkness. Thus, you should seek refuge against Satan. Ask Allah for His blessings and pray: 'O Allah take me away from darkness into the light and save me from all sort of foul deeds, whether they are hidden or manifest.' Some fears prevent one from committing manifest [foul] deeds. There are many hidden foul deeds that affect a man and take him far away. For example, some wrong scenes, wrong films, nude films and such things that man may see and commit fornication of the eye. There is also fornication of thoughts, reading wrong types of books or having such thoughts. Sitting in certain environments

pushes man into such foul deeds. There is also listening to foul deeds through the ears. Hence, we have been taught this prayer: 'O Allah with your blessing purify our organ. And keep it pure and make us among those who do not follow Satan and save us all from walking on the path of Satan."

- Friday Sermon Delivered 12 December 2003 at Baitul Futuh Mosque, London
- Published AlFazl International 06 February 2004

****

How can Waqfeen-e-Nau and Waqifat-e-Nau Attain Special Status?

- Become Special through Establishing High Standards
- Avoid Immorality
- Gain Education in Media
- Regularly listen to Friday Sermons on MTA

How can Waqfeen-e-Nau and Waqifat-e-Nau Attain Special Status?

Become Special through establishing high standards

On various occasions, Huzoor-e-Anwar (aba) has drawn the attention of parents of the Waqfeen-e-nau and Waqifat-e-nau towards the important obligation of training their children due to the honor that has been bestowed on them of offering their children in the way of Allah the Exalted. Parents of Waqfeen-e-nau should always remember that Jama'at has entrusted these children to them. Our objective should be to train them from a young age so they can become useful members of the Jama'at and the society. In this regard, Huzoor-e-Anwar has given valuable advice in his sermons, addresses and special classes with Waqfeen-e-nau. In a Friday sermon he said:

"In another instance, His Holiness the Promised Messiah(as) has referred to Prophet Abraham (as) to further expound on faithfulness, having done so in the following manner by saying, "The path to earning nearness to God Almighty demands the display of steadfastness." Stick to truthfulness, and ensure your faithfulness is sincere, "The nearness [to God] Prophet Abraham (as) acquired was due to this. Accordingly, Allah says:

$$ وَاِبْرٰهِيْمَ الَّذِيْ وَفّٰى ٥ $$

'And of Abraham who fulfilled the commandments?' [Holy Quran 53:38].

That, 'He was that Abraham who displayed faithfulness.' Demonstrating faithfulness, steadfastness, and sincerity to God demands a kind of death. Unless a person is prepared to extinguish his attachment to the world and all its pleasures and attractions and endure every humiliation and hardship for God, this quality cannot be developed. Idolatry is not merely that a person worships a tree or stone, rather every single thing, which prevents one from earning nearness to God and is preferred over Him is an idol; and man harbors these idols within himself to the extent that he is not even aware that he is worshipping idols." Frequently today, dramas [TV programs] have become idols, as has the Internet and pursuits of this world. In other instances, desires [have become idols]. Then, [the Promised Messiah (as)] states that a person is not even aware that he is worshipping idols while he is doing so within the depths of his being. Thus, [the Promised Messiah as] states, "Therefore, unless one sincerely becomes God's and is prepared to endure every hardship in His Way, the manifestation of steadfastness and sincerity is difficult." He continues, "Did Abraham as easily acquire this title from God? No. His announcement declaring:

$$ وَ اِبْرٰهِيْمَ الَّذِىْ وَفّٰى o $$

'And of Abraham who fulfilled the commandments?' [Holy Quran 53:38].

and came when he was ready to sacrifice his son. Allah desires actions and actions alone please Him and actions arise from pain." 'Actions arise from pain,' i.e., sacrifice is necessary for one's acts to be pious and earn Allah's pleasure. One has to expose oneself voluntarily to pain and sadness. But that person is not permanently in pain. Of course, pain is intertwined with such actions, but that person is not forever afflicted with pain. [The Promised Messiah (as)] states, "But when a person is prepared to endure pain for God's sake then God does not expose him to such pain...when Abraham (as) made all the preparations to sacrifice his son to fulfill God's commandment, then Allah the Almighty saved his son." The son's life was saved, and the father was saved from the pain that would have been experienced as a result of the sacrifice. [The Promised Messiah(as)] states, "He [Prophet Abraham (as)] was thrown into the fire, but the fire could not harm him in any manner." [The Promised Messiah (as)] states that if a person, "is prepared to endure pain for God's sake, God Almighty saves him from that pain."{Malfuzat, vol. 4, pg. 429-430, ed. 1985, England}".

Then Huzoor (aba) said:

"Briefly, I wish to draw attention to some Waqfeen administrative issues and procedures. Some people have raised the issue that some Waqfeen-e-Nau have a misconception in their minds that, upon becoming a member of Waqf-e-Nau, they have acquired a separate identity. They do have a distinct identity, but this does not afford them any extraordinary treatment. Rather, along with this identity, they will be expected to increase their level of sacrifice. Some people plant the idea in Waqfeen-e-Nau children that they are very special children, resulting in them feeling they are special when they become adults. And here as well, I have been made aware of instances where such individuals ignore the reality of waqf while making the purpose of their life to have the mere title of Waqf-e-Nau, believing it to make them special."

He further said:

"As I have said, Waqfeen-e-Nau are very special but to be special, they must demonstrate. What must they demonstrate? That they have excelled others regarding their relation with God Almighty—then they will be deemed special. That they have more fear of God than of anything else—then they will be deemed special. That the standards of their worship are far higher to that of others—then they will be deemed special. That, along with the fard [obligatory] prayers, they will observe nawafil [supererogatory] prayers—then they will be deemed special. That their overall moral standard is extremely high—this is one sign of them being special. That in their speech and actions, and their discussions, they are very different from others. It becomes clear that one with refined morals and one who, in every circumstance, gives precedence to faith over the world is one who will be deemed special. If they are female, their clothing and purdah should be an example of proper Islamic teachings which elicit envy from others and admissions that, truly, despite living in [Western] society their standard of clothing and purdah is extraordinary—then they are special. If they are male, then, due to modesty, they restrain their eyes and do not look waywardly—then they are special. Instead of looking at useless things on the Internet and the like, they spend such time only to acquire religious knowledge—then they are special. If the physical appearance of males is such that they are distinguishable from others, then they are special."

- Friday Sermon Delivered 28 October 2016 at Baitul Islam Mosque, Toronto
- Published AlFazl International 18 November 2016

Avoid immorality

Immoral actions are not only sins and make one go astray but they also lead to bad effects on human nature. In this regard, Huzoor-e-Anwar gave some important instructions to Waqfeen-e-Nau:

"Another sign of a believer is that he stays away from indecent and immoral things. During youth, there is a risk, particularly when living in this Western society that a person can be exposed to indecency and be led astray. For example, immoral and indecent programs are routinely shown on the TV and on the Internet. These are obscene and sinful things that a believer must stay far away from. Certainly, a Waqf-e-Nau who has renewed the pledge made by his parents prior to his birth to spend his entire life serving his faith must always stay away from such immoral activities. Allah the Almighty has said such things take people away from their faith and so true believers must save themselves from such indecency and all forms of wrongdoing."

- Address at National Waqf-e-Nau Ijtema 28 February 2016 Baitul Futuh Mosque, London
- Published AlFazl International 12 August 2016

Gain Education in Media

Media is expanding internationally; hence, Ahmadis should

pay special attention to gaining expertise in this field. Huzoor-e-Anwar (aba) has repeatedly drawn attention of the Waqfeen-e-nau and Waqifat-e-nau on playing an important role in the field of media, preparing experts in media for future needs of Jama'at in this field. On one occasion, he said:

"We also require people with media and communication related degrees and training. The work of MTA continues to expand and we have also started our radio service, Voice of Islam, recently. The radio is currently in its formative stage, but we wish to constantly develop it and increase its scope and we will require suitable manpower. Thereafter apart from MTA International, other local MTA studios are either being opened or are currently being developed in a number of countries. Thus, those of you who have a talent and interest in these fields, should pursue broadcasting, media and other similar technical fields. We also require journalists and media professionals, because the impact of the mass media is ever-increasing. And so, we need our people who can present the true teachings of Islam to the world through the media. Therefore, as Waqfeen-e-Nau, you should keep in mind what the requirements and needs of our Jama'at are, and based on those requirements, you should educate yourselves and work as hard as you can. Once you have completed your respective degrees or training, you should make sure you inform the Jama'at and submit yourselves as Waqf-e-Zindagi (a life devotee) and be ready to serve."

- Address at National Waqfe Nau Ijtema 28 February 2016 Baitul Futuh Mosque, London
- Published AlFazl International 12 August 2016

One day before giving the preceding address on this important topic, Huzoor-e-Anwar (aba) addressed the Annual Ijtema of the Waqifat-e-nau and said:

"I wish to say that within our Jama'at there is a particularly strong need for Ahmadi women doctors and teachers. Also, we require media graduates who can work in MTA or in any other way. And we also need Ahmadi journalists. Thus, those of you who have interests in these fields should try to pursue such avenues and paths."

- Address at National Waqifat-e-Nau Ijtema 27 February 2016 Baitul Futuh Mosque, London

Regularly listen to Friday Sermons on MTA

Words of the Khalifa of the time guarantee the establishment of a spiritual life and a source of reformation and training of future generations. Drawing the attention especially of the Waqfeen and Waqifat-e-nau towards listening to the Friday sermons, Huzoor-e-Anwar (aba) said:

"At the very least, they are to listen regularly to my sermons on MTA. And this instruction is not only important for the parents of Waqfeen-e-Nau but for every Ahmadi Muslim who wishes their progeny to stay attached to Nizam-e-Jama'at. They should make their homes Ahmadi Muslim homes, not worldly-minded homes. Otherwise, future generations will, having been absorbed in the material world, not only become distant from Ahmadiyyat but from God Almighty and this will destroy their life in this world and the next.

May God make it so that not only Waqfeen-e-Nau children earn God Almighty's nearness and act according to the dictates of taqwa [righteousness], but also that the conduct of their relatives be such that it saves them from every kind of disgrace. In fact, let it be that every Ahmadi Muslim become a true Ahmadi Muslim regarding whom the Promised Messiah (as) has repeatedly given instructions so that the raising of the flag of Ahmadiyyat and true

Islam can rapidly be seen."

- Friday Sermon Delivered 28 October 2016 at Baitul Islam Mosque, Toronto
- Published AlFazl International 18 November 2016

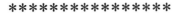

****

Lies and Deceit through Media

- **Fake Facebook Accounts**
- **Destruction through Cyber Attacks**
- **Deceit through letting someone use mobile phone**
- **Inappropriate use of the pictures of the Khulafa and avoiding innovations**

Lies and Deceit through Media

Fake Facebook Accounts

These days, Media is not only used for trampling upon all types of morality, but people are also using it to cheat and harm others through fraud and deception. Instructing Jama'at members to safeguard themselves, Huzoor-e-Anwar (aba) said:

"The third thing I want to say is that it has come to my knowledge that someone has created a Facebook [page] in my name. Someone created a Facebook account without my awareness. I have neither created this account, nor am I interested in creating one. In fact, a little while ago I had warned the Jama'at to avoid Facebook. There are many harms associated with it. I do not know whether someone made a silly mistake, whether an opponent did it, or some Ahmadi did it thinking he was committing a good act. Whatever the reason may be, we are trying to close the account and, Inshallah, it will be closed. There are more harms and less benefits in it.

I have individually been saying to people that Facebook leads to wrong actions and can be a source of worry for an individual. Girls need to be extremely careful in this regard. However, I want to make an announcement that you should ignore this Facebook [page] and no one should join it. People with Facebook accounts are visiting the page, reading it and commenting on it. This is wrong.

If a need arises for an official site like a Facebook page at a Jama'at level, we will create one in a secure way which cannot be accessed by everyone. It should just reflect Jama'at viewpoints and can be visited by anyone. I have been told that opponents [of the Jama'at] had commented [on the Facebook page]. It is an immoral act to create a Facebook page in someone else's name without telling the person, even if it is done with good intention.

Thus, whoever did it with good intention should immediately close it and offer Istighfār (repentance) and if it was created with ill-intent then Allah will deal with him. May Allah the exalted save us from all harm and may the Jama'at tread on the paths leading to progress."

- Friday Sermon Delivered 31 December 2010 at Baitul Futuh Mosque, London
- Published AlFazl International 21 January 2011

Destruction through Cyber Attacks

In a Friday sermon, Huzoor-e-Anwar (aba) mentioned the tense relations between various countries and his concern over new ways of harming each other, he said:

"Then, there are new inventions. Humans have created easier ways to communicate, keep records, [manage] economy, and oversee systems. Computers can manage many tasks. However, these new innovations can lead to the destruction of the world. These days cyber-attacks are occurring in certain countries and sometimes all over the world. These destroy entire systems. Even here [England], the NHS system was destroyed. Systems of airports were destroyed. These cyber-attacks can lead to escalating tensions with catastrophic results, lead to wars, and lead to destruction. A NATO representative has explained that if there was a cyber-attack on NATO [alliance] or other sensitive systems in the world, then it can lead to a destructive war and we cannot afford a dangerous attack like that. They have given this warning! Thus, the world is creating means of its own destruction. They think that progress of the worldly people is a source for its protection. This itself can lead to destruction. The worldly people and worldly government leaders are oblivious to this because of their own selfish gains. Especially when the president of the largest apparent power in the world sits within his own shell and makes fantastical claims that the world will act according to his wishes. These things are further deteriorating the situation. One thing is clear that due to his arrogance he is determined to destroy every opponent, and due to his hatred of Muslims, destroy all Muslims as well. He is determined to eliminate all opponents no matter who they are. He is oblivious to the fact even he will not be safe from the dangerous results of the world resulting from various causes."

- Friday Sermon Delivered 30 June 2017 at Baitul Futuh Mosque, London
- Published AlFazl International 21 July 2017

Deceit through letting someone use mobile phone

One may lend one's phone to a known or unknown person to help him, but such an act can be dangerous. Syria has been mired in internal strife for a long time; an innocent Ahmadi from Syria was a victim of deceit. Announcing his funeral prayers, Huzoor-e-Anwar (aba) said:

"Next, I will lead the funeral prayer in absentia of Abdul Noor Jabi Sahib of Syria. He was born in 1989. Perhaps he was arrested by the local government. A detailed description is not available. Based on the few details that I have, a few months ago he received his degree from a business management university. He was arrested by government agents on 31 Dec 2013. The reason was that someone borrowed his phone to make a call to the rebels. This happened during the initial days of the unrest in Syria. Lending your phone to some at the time of need is not objectionable. Anyhow, one of the rebels took his phone and discussed some financial matters with his companions. Phones are intercepted and checked by governmental agencies for such matters. They arrested him and the investigation established that the call was made from his phone and he was in touch with the rebels. For this reason, he was arrested and then martyred. According to the medical report, he died three days after the arrest due to a severe blow to his head. The government police officers use torture. The condition of the government agents is the same as that of the rebels. The news of his death reached his family on 22 February 2016. Inna lillahe wa inna Ilaihe rajioon [To Allah we belong and to Him is the return]."

- Friday Sermon Delivered 18 March 2016 at Baitul Futuh Mosque, London
- Published AlFazl International 08 April 2016

Inappropriate use of the pictures of the Khulafa and avoiding innovations

Huzoor-e-Anwar (aba) advised the Jama'at against the dangerous effect of innovation through the spread of the sharing pictures (such as those used on Social Media). On one occasion he said:

"Hazrat Musleh Maud (ra) narrated an incident that the Promised Messiah (as) had his photograph taken. However, when a postcard was presented to him which had his photo on it, he said that this could not be allowed. He instructed the community that no one should purchase those cards. As a result, no one dared to repeat this. (from Khutbat-e Mahmood vol 14 page 214)

These days, however, I have noticed on some tweets and on Whatsapp that some people are trying to circulate that old post card. They have either acquired it from an elder, or purchased it from a shop that sells old books. This is wrong and should be stopped. The Promised Messiah (as) had his photograph taken so that people from far-off places, especially Europeans who could judge a character from facial characteristics, would see it and it would lead them to seek the truth. However, when the Promised Messiah (as) saw that people may turn this into a business and sell his photograph on postcards, he felt this may become a source of harmful innovation and he strictly forbade it. In some instances, he asked for the postcards to be destroyed. **People who** have businesses selling photographs and charge exorbitant prices should pay attention to the matter. Some colorize photographs of the Promised Messiah (as); although, no color photograph of him exists. This is completely wrong and should also be avoided. Also, incorrect use of photographs of Khulafa should be avoided.

Once a debate on cinema and bioscope (movie camera) started at a Shura in front of Hazrat Musleh Maud (ra). He said it is incorrect to say that cinema, bioscope and phonograph in themselves were something bad. Indeed, the Promised Messiah (as) listened to a phonograph and even wrote a poem for it which he asked to be read and then invited the Hindus so that they could listen to it. This is the couplet from the poem:

This voice is coming from the phonograph

Seek God from the heart, not through boasting and bragging

Thus, cinema in itself is not bad (people constantly ask whether it is a sin to go there. It is not bad in itself) but these days what is projected through it, is immoral. There is nothing wrong with a film which has tabligh and educational aspects and has no element of 'show' (there should be no dramatization). He said 'putting on a show" etc. is wrong even when used for tabligh purposes. (from report of Majlise-mushawarat 1939, page 86)

This should clarify matters to those who suggest that it is alright if some music is used in MTA programs or it is acceptable if there is some music on Voice of Islam radio, a program that has recently launched. The Promised Messiah (as) had come to stop these harmful innovations and we have to mold our thoughts in accordance. It is neither forbidden, nor is it an innovation to take advantage of new inventions, but their wrong use makes them an innovation.

Some people are of the view that tabligh and tarbiyyat matters would be more impactful if there are presented in the form of a drama. It should always be remembered if you go down a wrong path or if you introduce something wrong in our program, then later a hundred harmful innovations will find their way. Some others might even think it is acceptable to recite the Holy Quran with music. However, an Ahmadi has to strive against these innovations. Hence, we should avoid such things and make a great effort to avoid such things."

He then said:

"A non-Ahmadi wrote in a newspaper something amusing which also reveals the ignorance of a Maulvi ['religious scholar']. It also shows their thinking regarding what they consider lawful. The author wrote that an Arab female singer was singing in Arabic. They took the Maulvi sahib there. He listened to the song while swaying [to her vocals]. He asked Maulvi sahib why are you swaying along with this Arab. [The maulvi] was also saying SubhanAllah and MashaAllah and Allah-o-Akbar. He replied, can you not see how beautifully she is reciting the Qur'an! As the song was in Arabic, he thought it was the Holy Quran. This is how thoughts change with the spread of harmful innovations."

- Friday Sermon Delivered 18 March 2016 at Baitul Futuh Mosque, London
- Published AlFazl International 08 April 2016

****

AL ISLAM
The Official Website of the Ahmadiyya Muslim Community

*Muslims who believe in the Messiah,
Hazrat Mirza Ghulam Ahmad Qadiani[as]*

He is Allah, the Creator, the Maker, the Fashioner, His are the most beautiful names. All that is in the heavens and the earth glorifies Him, and He is the Mighty, the Wise. (59:25)

ALLAH
Among Muslims, the name of the One, Supreme-Being also known as God. more...

• • • •

Noah's Ark

by The Promised Messiah[as]
view online

Pathway to Peace

by Hazrat Mirza Masroor Ahmad
view online

Friday Sermons
Recent Friday Sermon
Archive: [1899 - 2018]

Recent Additions & Highlights   » more recent additions

Audio Books   Listen to books using audio (mp3) books:
English Audio Books | Urdu Audio Books
Also available on **SoundCloud**

 Khilafat: Successorship to Prophethood
Learn about the history, significance and re-establishment of this divine institution. » more

The Grand Prophecy of the Eclipses
Learn more about this prophecy by reading a response to some recent allegations. » more

Islam
Islam is the religion that represents the pinnacle of religious evolution. » more

The Ahmadiyya Muslim Community
Ahmadiyyat is the revival of Islam prophesied to unite humanity in the Latter Days. » more

Allah
The name of the One, Supreme-Being also known as God in other faiths. » more

The Promised Messiah
Hazrat Mirza Ghulam Ahmad[as], the Promised Messiah and Mahdi. » more

The Holy Prophet
Hazrat Muhammad[sa], a Messenger of God and the Seal of the Prophets. » more

Hadhrat Mirza Masroor Ahmad[aba]
The Fifth Khalifa after the Promised Messiah. » more

Articles of Faith   Five Pillars
» Unity of God   » Kalima
» His Angels   » Prayer
» His Books   » Fasting
» His Prophets   » Zakaat
» The Last Day   » Hajj
» Divine Decree

The Tomb of Jesus
Recently discovered and preserved in Kashmir, India. » more

Selected Topics
» Character of Muhammad[sa]
» Muhammad in the Bible
» Jihad & Terrorism
» Women in Islam
» Prayer (Salaat) Guide
» more topics...

Selected Topics
» Khilafat
» Finality of Prophethood
» Return of Jesus
» Re-Institution of Khilafat
» Conditions of Initiation
» more topics...

Search Al Islam   Search

International
Islam
Ask Islam
Islamic FAQ
About Ahmadiyyat
Press Releases
Holy Quran
Ahadith
Ruhani Khaza'in
Library

العربية   أردو

Adhan   Salat
Urdu Poems   Al Fazl
Wallpapers   Apps
Media Library Photo Gallery

 **Muslim Television**
MTA3 قليل بعد...
السيرة المطهرة
» Watch MTA now

FRIDAY SERMONS
» Recent Friday Sermon
» Archive [1899 - 2018]

AL ISLAM LIBRARY
✦ Books   ✦ Articles
✦ Periodicals ✦ Multimedia
» more in the Al Islam Library

THE HOLY QURAN
Search Quran Translation
                    Search
advanced search arabic search
Browse Quran Translations
English   ▼ Go
» more about the Holy Quran

Al Islam Newsletter
Subscribe & view archives

Annual Conventions
■ Bangladesh Feb 2-4
■ Qadian, India Dec 29-31
■ USA West Coast Dec 22-24

An Extract from Friday Sermon by Hazrat Khalifatul Masih V (aba)

"...It is neither forbidden, nor is it an innovation to take advantage of new inventions, but their wrong use makes them an innovation."

(Friday Sermon Delivered 18 March 2016 at Baitul Futuh Mosque, London)

Benefits of Social Media

- **Blessings of MTA**
- **MTA is a means to connect with Khilafat**
- **Tabligh through MTA**
- **Opposition cannot hinder the progress of Jama'at**
- **Message of Islam through the publication, "Review of Religions"**
- **Alislam.org an important tool for propagation of Islam**
- **Friday Sermon: a spiritual blessing**
- **Allah's promises will come to fruition**
- **'And by those who spread a thorough spreading'**

وَّ النّٰشِرٰتِ نَشْرًا

(Holy Qur'an 77:4)

Benefits of Social Media

Huzoor-e-Anwar has repeatedly drawn attention to using innovation in communication to strengthen our relationship with religion so that we may gain benefit from the educational and spiritual treasures. These worldly resources are bringing precious souls to the right path leading to Islam.

Blessings of MTA

Muslim Television Ahmadiyya is a source of religious treasure whose blessings are reaching the corners of the earth. Instructing to gain benefit from it, Huzoor-e-Anwar (aba) said:

"Thus, in the current era media has brought us closer to each other not just within a country but around the world. Unfortunately, rather than bringing us closer to virtues, it has brought us closer to following Satan. Under such circumstances, an Ahmadi should be extremely watchful of his own state. Allah the Exalted has bestowed MTA on us. Allah the Exalted has given us a website for spiritual and educational programs of Jamā'at. We can only stay focused on it if we pay full attention to it. This will take us near to God and we will be saved from Satan."

- Friday Sermon delivered 20 May 2016 at Gottenberg Mosque, Sweden
- Published AlFazl International 10 June 2016

Our leader Hazrat Ameerul Momineen Hazrat Khalifatul Masih V (aba) sent a message to the members of the Jama'at at the occasion of Annual Jalsa Salana Australia held in December 2015. It concluded in these words:

"I have repeatedly drawn the attention of Ahmadis all around the world to watch programs on MTA. Parents should pay attention to this, as well as making sure their children are attached to MTA. This is a spiritual blessing which is the source of your spiritual survival. It will increase your religious knowledge. You will make spiritual progress and have a strong connection with Khilafat. It will also save you from the toxic effect of other worldly channels. May Allah enable you to act on my advice. Ameen"

- Message for Jalsa Salana Australia 24 December 2015
- Published AlFazl International 15 July 2016

On one occasion advising Lajna Ima'illah to gain maximum blessings from MTA, Huzoor-e-Anwar (aba) said:

"As I have said today we are able to utilize modern technology to convey our teachings. Apart from MTA we also have Jama'at websites through which programs and books filled with knowledge and information are easily available. You must seek to avail these resources and constantly increase in your knowledge. In terms of MTA, **every Lajna member should attach themselves to it and be regular in watching its programs. At the very least they should ensure they watch my Friday Sermons and the other programs of Khalifatul Masih. And they should make sure their children also sit and listen.** Those girls who have grown up here in the UK should also ensure they are closely attached to MTA and the Jama'at websites. They should make sure they watch the programs of Khalifa of the time as this will be the means of their spiritual and moral development and will increase their religious knowledge.

In all parts of the world people are joining the fold of Ahmadiyyat having recognized its truth by watching MTA. For example, recently a man from an extremely tiny and remote island near France wrote that somehow, he had come across MTA and my sermon was being broadcast. In the sermon I spoke about the death of Jesus Christ (as) and after listening to it the man said he was quite certain it was the correct teaching. He then went on the Internet to research the Jama'at and watched our programs on YouTube. And after doing so he said he was sure of the truth of Ahmadiyyat. And so, with the Grace of Allah he did Bai'at. There are also many Ahmadi women who join our Jama'at and are extremely strong in their faith."

- Address at Annual Ijtema Lajna Ima'illah UK 25 October 2015
- Published AlFazl International 25 March 2016

MTA is a means to connect with Khilafat

Muslim Television Ahmadiyya is a great blessing from which every advantage should be taken. Huzoor-e-Anwar (aba) said:

"These days, as presented through earlier examples, many things lead to the displeasure of God. Correct use of these things is not bad; however, their incorrect use leads to spread of foulness, evil and sin. However, the same thing can also be a means of spreading goodness. Television can be a source of knowledge and education, but it can also spread indecency. In these current times, Ahmadiyya Jama'at and Ahmadis are making the best use of the television. I had drawn attention to watching MTA during the days of the Jalsa, and this influenced some people. They have said to me that they did not watch MTA before, but now because of your drawing of our attention to it, we have started watching it. They are now expressing regret to me for not watching MTA before and being connected to it and some say that even viewing it for just a week to ten days has improved their standard of spirituality and knowledge. They have learned about Jama'at.

Hence, I am reminding again that you should pay great attention in your homes to gain benefit from this blessing which Allah the Exalted has bestowed on us for our training and to increase our knowledge and spiritualty, so our generations may stay firm on Ahmadiyyat. Hence, we should try to connect ourselves to MTA. In addition to sermons, there are many live programs which can enhance religious knowledge and spirituality. The Jama'at spends hundreds of thousands of dollars every year [on MTA] for the training of the Jama'at members. If members of the Jama'at do not avail of it, it will be their own loss. Outsiders are gaining benefit from MTA and are realizing the truthfulness of the Jama'at and are knowing about and understanding the unity of Allah and the reality of Islam. Hence, Ahmadis in Australia and the rest of the world should gain maximum benefit from MTA. One of its blessings is that it is a great means to connect the Jama'at to the blessings of Khilafat. Hence, we must avail it."

- Friday sermon delivered 18 October 2013 at Baitul Huda Mosque, Sydney, Australia
- Published AlFazl International 08 November 2013

Huzoor-e-Anwar (aba) has spoken about tarbiyyat of Ahmadi Girls on numerus occasion. In this regard, he stated the following in a message:

"Lajna Ima'illah is one of the auxiliaries of the Jama'at and has a branch called Nasirat-ul-Ahmadiyya, which is the organization of Ahmadi girls up to the age of 15 years. Hence, due to the Grace of Allah you are part of a strong and active organizational structure of the Jama'at, whose mission is to inform the world of the teachings of Islam and Ahmadiyyat. Hence, it is essential for you to have a vast religious education. You should be familiar with your beliefs and be observant of Islamic teachings. For example, wear modest clothes, and once you reach the age of wearing a coat and burqa, do not leave home without it. Safeguard yourself against indecent gatherings, immoral friendships and from the evils of the Internet and mobile phones, etc.

In his book 'The Noah's Ark', Promised Messiah (as) has given stern warning to those who do not give up bad friends and bad gatherings. Hence, always remember this teaching.

Nasirat are in the age of acquiring education. Pay special attention to your education and work hard for a better future and turn to prayers. Adopt such activities that reflect your love for religion. For example, you should plan to listen to my sermon on Friday when it is broadcast on MTA. Make notes while doing so, so your full attention is focused on the sermons. If you do not understand some matters, ask your elders. This will establish your personal relations with the Khalifa of the time, increase your religious knowledge, purify your thoughts and ideas, and strengthen your passion to serve the religion and participate in Jama'at programs. Remember, the more you keep yourself closer to the faith, the more likely you are to safeguard yourself from socials evils. This will lead to peace of mind. If you do tabligh, it will have an impact."

- Message for Lajna Ima'illah Germany Published Monthly Magazine Guldasata 20 March 2017
- Published AlFazl International 09 June 2017

Tabligh through MTA

Through MTA progress of the Jama'at is demonstrated and regular programs are broadcast inviting to Allah and women are also benefitting from this. In this regard, Huzoor-e-Anwar (aba) said:

"Since I have talked about Allah's blessings and His making our work easy for us, I will give you a few examples of how He is opening up the hearts of the people, including women. I have taken the examples of few women whom Allah is including among those who are striving to fulfill the rights of being the Khair-e-Ummat (best of people). Halwaani Sahibah from Syria relates her dreams. In her first dream, she says that I saw a group of Ulema (religious scholars) who, it seemed, were sitting in Al Hawaar-ul-Mubaashir (which is one of our Arabic programs on MTA), and were sharing information about the life of the Promised Messiah (as). Upon waking up, I could only remember the word 'Punjab' which I had never heard before. I related this dream to an Ahmadi friend of mine and asked her the meaning of this word, who was astounded at hearing this. Sometime later, in a dream I saw a Noor (light) in the form of a person who was wearing a turban and sitting crossed-legged (on the floor) and telling me that he was the Mahdi. When I woke up, I was very happy and expressed my desire to take Bai'at (oath of initiation); but my Bai'at was delayed for some reason. Then she says, that I saw in a third dream that I was lying down during the day for rest, when a voice addressed me saying that 'I am telling you for the third time that I am the Mahdi, who are you waiting for?' After this my daughter woke me up and I felt both astonished and worried. Therefore, I quickly did Bai'at.

- Address at Annual Ijtema Lajna Ima'illah Germany at Manheim, Germany 17 September 2011
- Published AlFazl International 16 November 2012

Huzoor-e-Anwar (aba) explained how a young African man loved MTA and gained benefits from it:

"I will present the example of a young man named Bassam who lived in a city in Ivory Coast. He said that he was a non-Ahmadi Muslim and was greatly interested in Islam. He attended non-Ahmadi mosques; however, those Muslims were engaged in personal conflict. This broke his heart, causing him grief and sorrow. After a while, by Allah's Grace he was introduced to Ahmadiyya Jama'at. Hence, he started offering his Salat in our mosque and would listen to local Dars-ul-Quran. Local Ahmadis continued to preach to him. Very quickly, he understood the truthfulness of Ahmadiyyat, and he took the Bai'at. He did not just limit it to performing the Bai'at, and he did not consider taking the Bai'at to be enough. Instead, he diligently watched MTA in the local mosque. As a result of watching MTA, he was so impressed by it that he saved money and within a few months installed a satellite dish in his house. He said that his faith increased as he continued watching programs about Ahmadiyya Jama'at. He is French speaking, yet he also watched programs that were not in the French language. He has memorized the complete schedule of MTA. He said that my sermons and other such programs are a special source of contentment for his heart. **Thus, every Ahmadi Muslim should recognize the blessing of Allah in the form of MTA and we should not be ungrateful for it.**

As prophesized by the Holy Prophet (saw), the world passed through many phases and now it has entered the everlasting Khilafat of Islam that Allah had prophesied. Hence, every Ahmadi should strengthen his connection and relation with Khilafat and follow in the footsteps of the young man from Ivory coast. He also said that he has not missed any Friday sermon of Hazrat Khalifatul Masih (aba) or any program of Hazrat Khalifatul Masih (aba) and has watched every program. He always finds points that increase his faith. Thus, every young Ahmadi should change his priorities and be really grateful for the blessing of Allah in the form of MTA. We should connect with MTA. With the Grace of Allah, MTA is preparing great programs on many topics in light of current situations and affairs. You should watch these programs to understand the Islamic perspective on different affairs and issues, so that your religious knowledge may increase. And in this manner, Inshallah, your bond with Islam and Ahmadiyyat will increase."

- Address at National Ijtema Khuddam ul Ahmadiyya UK 14 June 2015, Tilford, Surrey
- Published AlFazl International 14 April 2017

Like many others, an Arab accepted Islam Ahmadiyyat through MTA. Mentioning this incident Huzoor-e-Anwar said:

"Ahmad sahib from Jordan says that he was introduced to the Jama'at through MTA. Being satisfied by the perspectives that he heard through it, he was content and prayed to Allah for guidance. He says that after he prayed, he saw a dream where he saw a man who was standing on a rooftop calling the Fajr adhan. After completing the adhan he said: 'Hayya Alal Ahmadiyya

Hayya Alal Ahmadiyya meaning come to Ahmadiyyat, come to Ahmadiyyat. The Muazzin [one who calls the Adhan] also said some other sentences in my dream, but I only remember this. The strange thing is that as I woke up, the neighborhood Muazzin was calling the Adhan. After this clear dream I decided to take the pledge.' Hence, he did Bai'at along with his sons and other family members."

- Address at Jalsa Salana UK 13 August 2016
- Published AlFazl International 20 January 2017

Speaking about a spiritual change due to MTA, Huzoor-e-Anwar (aba) said:

"Amir Sahib Gambia writes that in the village Mamt Fanna, the Maulawis led a severe opposition to the Jama'at. People in the village who had accepted Ahmadiyyat installed MTA and started watching the programs. As a result, people's interest in Ahmadiyyat continued to increase. Gradually, the opponents also started watching programs on MTA. When people who were severely opposed to the Jama'at listened to the sermons, they said this person should not be opposed. It is said that 350 people accepted Ahmadiyyat.

Amir Sahib Gambia writes that a woman in the village Mamt Fanna accepted Ahmadiyyat and started watching programs on MTA. Her husband was strongly opposed to Ahmadiyyat. Once when she spoke about the Jama'at and Khilafat at home, her husband became furious and said that after today no one will talk about Ahmadiyyat in our home. He scolded his wife in front of other people. She listened to her husband calmly and patiently. However, she remained steadfast on Ahmadiyyat and continued to watch MTA. After a while, the husband also started watching MTA. As a result, one month later, her husband also accepted Ahmadiyyat."

- Address at Jalsa Salana UK 22 August 2015
- Published AlFazl International 12 February 2016

Opposition cannot hinder the progress of Jama'at

Opponents of the Jama'at think that they can stop the tabligh efforts (preaching) by imposing a ban on our books and magazines. However, through other means of media, Allah the Exalted is spreading the message of Ahmadiyyat to the corners of the earth. Huzoor-e-Anwar (aba) explained the action of the government of Punjab to ban books, and said:

"Last Friday, I had mentioned that the government of Punjab [in Pakistan] has recently banned the publication and display of some Jama'at magazines and books. Some newspapers there have published this news. These days, news spreads around the world in minutes using mobile phone through images, messages and other methods of communications. After seeing and hearing this, people write to me also. Through fax and other means of communications, they convey their worry. We should remember that this is nothing new. Throughout the history of the Jama'at, so-called religious leaders have done similar actions and will continue to do so. Their ploys did not harm the Jama'at in the past, and Inshallah they will not harm it in future. And they cannot cause any harm! No mother has given birth to a child who can stop the divine mission of the Promised Messiah (as). The so-called religious scholars and their supportive governments need a way to display the jealousy they have at the progress of the Jama'at and the intensity of their jealousy makes them lose their senses. Apparently educated folk behave worse than illiterates, without trying to find out the glorious manner in which the Promised Messiah (as) wrote about the real teachings of Islam and about the status and glory of Holy Prophet (saw). The literature of the Jama'at presents this beautifully. Fair-minded people, whether Arabs or from other nations, are astonished when they witness the reality and see the books and literature of the Jama'at. Then, they realize the utterly false and fabricated manner in which the perspective, teachings, and writings of the Promised Messiah (as) are portrayed and continued to be portrayed by these so-called religious leaders who call themselves the flag bearers of Islam. They see how the Promised Messiah (as) has explained the status of the Holy Prophet (saw) and the grandeur of the beautiful teaching of Islam. People now have accepted Ahmadiyyat and those who have not yet done so, write letters or call into our live programs and say that we have only now realized this status and grandeur [of the Holy Prophet]. We were kept ignorant by these 'scholars.' These people realize that due to their animosity against Ahmadiyyat intentionally or unintentionally these people level objections on Islam and the Holy Prophet (saw).

Regardless, this animosity and turmoil is the religion of these scholars. Therefore, they will never try to know the facts, no matter how much chaos is created for simple Muslims. Anyway, these are their ways and they will keep on acting in this manner because their personal benefits are dearer to them than their religion. However, as always, the actions of these opponents should rekindle our faith and strengthen our relationship with the Promised Messiah (as). If we did not pay attention towards reading the books of the Promised Messiah (as), then now we should instill a stronger desire [to read the books of the Promised Messiah (as)] in ourselves.

These works can neither be stopped by a ban imposed by the government of Punjab nor by any ban of any other government because [these] works are not due to human effort. These works are from Allah the Exalted. He sent the Promised Messiah (as) with the treasures of knowledge and wisdom, and promised victory to him. We have always seen that the Jama'at has always had greater victories in the face of strong obstacles and opposition. This is an insignificant obstacle raised against us, an action stemming from their arrogance. The more we are suppressed, the more we receive grace from Allah. Inshallah, good things will happen. So, we should not worry about this.

The books of the Promised Messiah (as) are being printed in other countries of the world. They are available on websites. Some are available as audio books and others will, Inshallah, soon be made available [in this format]. There was a time when a ban on publications would have been a cause of concern. **Now these treasures of knowledge and wisdom have been spread to the skies and come in front of us at the push of a button. It is our job to reap the greatest benefits from the knowledge, sayings, and writings of the Promised Messiah (as).** I have decided to increase the time of dars [lecture] on the books of the Promised Messiah (as). In this way, Ahmadis who are impacted due to the law in one province will benefit. Each obstacle, each opposition benefits us and draws our attention to new ways and means. Inshallah, it will be such that not only will these books be published and lectures will be delivered on them in local languages, but this material will be available in local languages of many nations. People have been writing to me, hence I have to say this, those who have any kind of worry in their hearts must remove it."

- Friday Sermon Delivered at Baitul Futuh Mosque London 15 May 2015
- Published AlFazl International 05 June 2015

Message of Islam through the publication, "Review of Religions"

In 1902, the Promised Messiah (as) started a magazine from Qadian in Urdu and English for preaching Islam among the English-speaking world. This [magazine] is spreading the Noor (light) of Islam to the intellectual readers of the world in English, German, and French through print and electronic media. Mentioning this magazine in an address, Huzoor-e-Anwar said:

"Review of Religions was started by the Promised Messiah (as) in 1902, 114 years ago. With the grace of Allah, it comes out in multiple formats through the latest means and resources. With the grace of Allah, the message of Islam is being shared with a large number through the print edition of this magazine, website, Social Media, YouTube and other exhibitions. Through these various platforms more than a million people received the message of Islam."

- Address at Jalsa Salana UK 13 August 2016 at Hadiqatul Mahdi, Alton
- Published AlFazl International 20 January 2017

Alislam.org an important tool for propagation of Islam

Important material for tabligh and tarbiyyat has been presented in various languages on the website: Alislam.org. Only those people who utilize this website understand its benefit. A team of volunteers continually work to improve this website. Mentioning this website in a Friday sermon, Huzoor-e-Anwar said:

"There is one more thing that I want to mention. I wanted to mention this at the end of the Jalsa in Qadian. With Allah's grace we have a new resource on our website, alislam. Rohani Khazain' which are the books by the Promised Messiah (as) have been added to a search engine. If you want to find something and you enter a word, for example, Allah or Jesus the Messiah or Muhammad (saw) then, wherever this word has been used in the volumes of 'Ruhani Khaza'in will display in the form of name and reference. Then, you can see the pages that were the actual pages of the book through searching the Internet or on Alislam. This is a great accomplishment and was a difficult task. With the grace of Allah, a team of our youth has accomplished this."

He then said:

"Thus, they accomplished a huge task. The ones using this may not appreciate it. These young men did a lot of work by reading each book, finding each word in the book, then making an index, and then making a program for the index and the pages. May Allah reward them and may the world reap benefit from it.

Those who want to object, will keep objecting against the books of the Promised Messiah (as). However, if you see, this is a treasure which can be a source of reformation for this world. Those who do not care, even make fun of the verses of the Holy Quran. May Allah the Exalted give wisdom and understanding to the world."

- Friday Sermon 31 December 2010 at Baitul Futuh Mosque, London
- Published AlFazl International 21 January 2011

Friday Sermon: a spiritual blessing

In the concluding address to the Majlis Shura Jama'at-e-Ahmadiyya UK, Huzoor-e-Anwar (aba) advised the members of the Shura to gain maximum benefit from MTA, especially regularly listening to the Friday sermon. Huzoor-e-Anwar (aba) said:

"One other matter that I want to especially draw the attention of the office holders and delegates of Majlis Shura is that you and your family members should gain maximum benefit from MTA, as much as possible. You should also encourage other friends to gain benefit from MTA. Initially, you should set aside some time each day for watching programs of your interest on MTA. For example, those friends who want to listen to the English program would find excellent English programs that are broadcast on a daily basis. They should regularly listen to those programs.

The most important need of the times is that you should regularly listen to the Friday sermon which is broadcast each Friday. Then, you should also watch such programs that I attend, for example addresses to non-Muslims, my speeches at Jalsa, or other occasions. Inshallah, watching such programs will be beneficial for you and you should watch these programs for this reason."

- Concluding Address Majlis-e-Shura UK 16 June 2013 at Baitul Futuh Mosque, London
- Published AlFazl International 25 October 2013

At the concluding address of the National Ijtema of Waqfeen-e-nau Jama'at Ahmadiyya UK, Huzoor gave much important advice on various topics. In this address, Huzoor gave special instruction to gain benefit from the Friday sermon because it can be a source of creating a strong bond of the members of the Jama'at with the Khalifa of the time. Huzoor-e-Anwar said:

"You should also have complete belief in the fact that Allah the Almighty has provided the means and resources in this era, the era of the Promised Messiah (as), to complete the propagation of Islam. At the time of the Holy Prophet (saw), the Law had reached its perfection and thus he (saw) was the Khatamun Nabiyyin, the Seal of all the Prophets. However, the means to spread the message to all parts of the world had not yet appeared, such as the media and other forms of spreading the message. At the time of the Promised Messiah (as), in accordance with the promises of Allah the Almighty, additional means and resources became available such as mass media, television, press and so on, which provided the platform for the message of Islam to reach from one corner of the world to the other. With the Grace of Allah the Almighty, today the Ahmadiyya Jama'at has been given these means by Allah the Almighty to spread Islamic teachings to the world. Thus, it is the duty of every member of the Jama'at, whichever part of the world they live in, to make full and proper use of these modern means and resources. They should strive to propagate the message of Islam in all directions and in all parts of the world and, thus, partake of the blessings which Allah the Almighty has conferred upon us in this era."

Mentioning the use of the latest technology to get direct benefit from the Friday sermons, Huzoor-e-Anwar said:

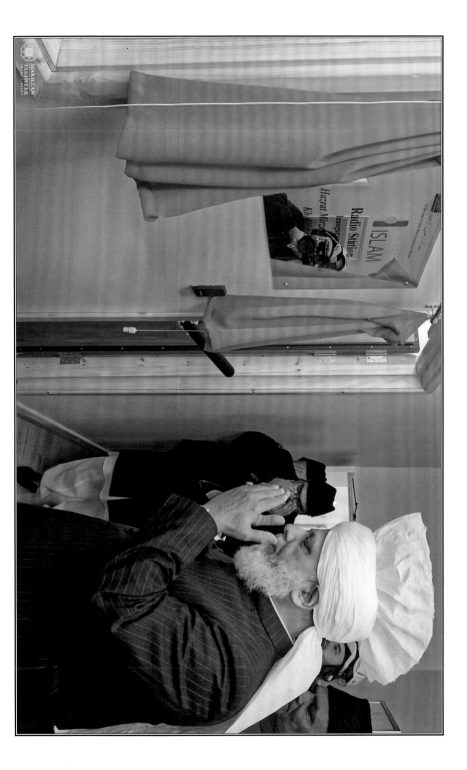

"Further, you should also have absolute belief and conviction that after the demise of the Promised Messiah (as), in accordance with the promise of Allah the Almighty and the prophecies of the Holy Prophet (saw), the real and true system of Khilafat has been established, which you must obey and follow fully. A very important means of fulfilling obedience to Khilafat and implementing the guidance of the Khalifa is in the shape of the great favor and blessing Allah the Almighty has established for us through MTA. Therefore, through MTA you should make every possible effort to regularly listen to my Sermons wherever you may be, whether through the TV, Computer, Laptop or mobile phone. In this era no one can justifiably make the excuse that they were unable to receive the message or teachings, as through the media and other means everything is now easily and readily available to us at the click of a button. And so, in terms of the Sermons they can also be accessed easily in many different ways. You can watch the sermons on MTA through TV, or you can download it from the MTA website or watch it through the MTA OnDemand service. There are also other programs on MTA which are important for you to watch as they will enhance your religious knowledge and will also be a source of strengthening your bond with Khilafat. Another means of increasing your religious knowledge is also through the Alislam website, where a wide range of material is available. And so, as you have reached a mature age you should connect yourselves as much as possible to all these various resources and means. By doing so, while you should try to increase your knowledge, you should also use these means to strengthen your connection with Khilafat and discharge your responsibility of giving precedence to the faith over worldly affairs. Nowadays there are countless programs on TV and there are websites on the Internet or other things which draw a person's interest and attract his attention. Using them never comes to an end and so to say we have to finish or complete our worldly activities and engagements first and then watch MTA on TV or through streaming, will mean that in reality you will never find time to watch MTA. In order to discharge your responsibilities by benefitting from those means and resources that will enhance your religious knowledge, you will have to give precedence to your religion and faith over worldly programs and activities."

- National Waqfeen-e-Nau Ijtema UK 01 March 2015
- Published AlFazl International 22 July 2016

MTA is establishing a strong connection between members of the Jama'at and Khilafat-e-Ahmadiyya at an international level. Mentioning this, Huzoor (aba) said:

"In this age, Allah the Exalted has created further ease for us. For one, every Ahmadi should instil the practice of watching MTA for personal tarbiyyat and forging a strong connection with Khilafat. We should tell others about the programs on MTA and website. If you get an opportunity, sit with your friends and watch such programs. Introduce these to your friends. Many people write to say that ever **since they started regularly watching at least the Friday sermon on MTA they have strengthened their faith and feel their connection with Jama'at has also become stronger. Our faith is getting stronger.** Thus, MTA and the Alislam web site are both very good resources for tabligh about the Promised Messiah (as) and also resources for tarbiyyat of Ahmadis and connecting them to Khilafat and the Jama'at. It is obligatory on every Ahmadi to connect to these."

- Friday Sermon delivered 04 March 2016 Baitul Futuh Mosque, London
- Published AlFazl International 25 March 2016

In a Friday sermon, Huzoor-e-Anwar explained the benefit of Friday sermon with regards to reformation and improvement in the practice of the members of the community. He said:

"As said before, Khulafa-e-Ahmadiyyat have been drawing attention to improving the practice [of faith]. Through sermons and other writings, previous Khufala and I have been drawing attention to removing these shortcomings. Jama'at and the auxiliary organizations also make programs, in light of the guidance, to safeguard Ahmadis at all levels and for all ages against the attack of the enemy. However, each of us should tend to our own practical reformation, and firmly stand up to the enemies of faith; even more, stand firm to help reform these enemies because it is not enough to only stand guard against the enemy, but rather we should proactively help them reform. In order to accomplish this, if a personal relationship is established with God, then not only will we be able to defeat the enemy, but by reforming them their lives will improve in this life and the hereafter. We would also be destroying the fitna (trial) that is trying to influence our future generations. In this way we will defend our future generations. We will be safeguarding the faith of those who are weak amongst us. This practical reformation will spread from one to another and this will continue till the Day of Judgement. Our practical reformation will also open the ways for preaching. Instead of spreading evil, the new inventions will become a means of spreading the name of God in every region and country."

- Friday Sermon delivered 06 Dec 2013 Baitul Futuh Mosque, London
- Published AlFazl International 27 December 2013

Allah's promises will come to fruition

While electronics and Social Media has allowed great progress to be made in the matters of tabligh (preaching) and tarbiyyat (reformation), it has also allowed enemies of Ahmadiyyat to stir trouble. In this regard, Huzoor-e-Anwar (aba) said:

"There are many promises of Allah with the Promised Messiah (as) and InshAllah these promises will and are being fulfilled. I will relate a few incidents to you, which show how

Allah is expanding the Jama'at. However, I tell young girls in particular who are sometimes misled by the Internet or other people, [and feel] that the Jama'at is not progressing, or they despair and feel frustrated and the enemy tries to spread despair among us. Opponents make effort to do this and the same is done through the media now days, especially through vulgar discussions on websites etc. Slowly and gradually this creates despair in the minds of our youth, which makes them drift away from religion. Therefore, always be mindful of never entertaining any thought of frustration and despair."

- Address at the Annual Ijtema Lajna Ima'illah Germany 17 September 2011
- Published AlFazl International 16 November 2010

'And by those who spread a thorough spreading' [Wanashirati nashran] وَّ النّٰشِرٰتِ نَشۡرًا

Inventions of the current age and the latest means of communication are proving helpful and beneficial in spreading the true message of Islam. Huzoor-e-Anwar (aba) has repeatedly mentioned the supportive signs from Allah, rewards, and victories in Friday sermons and addresses. While explaining this topic with reference to the Holy Quran, he (aba) said:

"We should remember that the power of Allah the Exalted is not limited. If He so wills, He may grant fulfillment of all prophecies and victories made to a prophet during his lifetime. However, Allah desires that those coming later should also become a part of these victories and blessings. Hence, the high-speed resources of this age are drawing our attention to the fact that we should utilize them appropriately. We should use them and follow in the footstep of the Companions (may Allah be pleased with them). We should become supporters and helpers for the Leader (Imam) of the time and by becoming his helpers we may fulfill his mission. **Fast resources draw our attention**

to consider this speed as a blessing from God and utilize it for His faith.

Allah has said,

وَّ النّٰشِرٰتِ نَشۡرًا ۟

'And by those who spread a thorough spreading'
(Holy Quran 77:4)

And presented those who spread the message in a good manner as a witness. This is the message for which the Holy Prophet (saw) was appointed. It is the perfect religion that will last until the Day of Judgement, and in the current age, the advent of the Promised Messiah (as) occurred for its revival.

In this age, God has provided modern means of propagating this message. The Companions of the Holy Prophet (saw) did not have modern means and resources yet they honored the dues of tabligh. Today, the means and resources are available. They were destined for the time of the 'ardent devotee' of Holy Prophet (saw) and Allah had prophesied about these. This verse, which is a prophecy, is mentioned at another place [in the Qur'an] as:

وَ اِذَا الصُّحُفُ نُشِرَتۡ ۟

'And when books are spread.' (Holy Quran 81:11)

This era, which is the era of the Promised Messiah (as) is the era of the spread of books. For this reason, he has left an immense ocean of his writings, "Ruhani Khaza'in" (spiritual treasures), which were published during his lifetime. His companions played a great role in spreading these. We read, in the narratives of the companions, [many examples of] one of them giving a book to someone who was greatly influenced after reading the book. Many people entered Ahmadiyyat this way. People undertook this with a spirit of sacrifice just as the Companions in the first era of Islam did. And then these people, these Companions who have been presented as a witness, became the beloved of Allah the Exalted. Later, the companions of the Promised Messiah (as) also followed in the footsteps of the Companions of the Prophet Muhammad (saw) and these people also became the beloved of Allah the Exalted.

Today, Allah the Exalted has provided efficient means to spread these books and respond to the opponents of Islam. It used to take time to spread books, but now, a message can be delivered instantaneously. As soon as a book is published, it can be printed at the other end. These days, the books of the Promised Messiah (as), the Holy Quran, and other Islamic literature is traversing new stages of broadcast through Internet and television. The speed of media today could not have been imagined a few decades ago. Thus, avail these opportunities given to us by Allah the Exalted, for preaching and defense of Islam. **It is a favor of Allah the Exalted that he has provided these latest inventions in this time. By making these available the work of preaching has been made easier.** We should try to appropriately use these, instead of wasting time in frivolities and wrong activities. We should make use of these and if we become part of the group that is spreading the message of the Messiah of Muhammad (saw) to the world, then we can be considered part of this group. We can be those people by whom Allah bore witness.

I had said the same at the MTA event that today each worker of MTA, no matter where in the world he or she is working, is working to take the message of the Promised Messiah (as) to the ends of the earth. God will make this happen, He revealed to the Promised Messiah (as), 'I shall carry thy message to the ends of the earth' and for this purpose He provided these resources to spread [His] message to the ends of the earth. God has destined it to be so, and all the inventions bear witness to it.

- Friday Sermon delivered 15 October 2010 Baitul Futuh Mosque, London
- Published AlFazl International 05 November 2010

Rapid progress in modern forms of communication and

media industry has laid greater responsibilities on the Ahmadis. Explaining this topic, Huzoor (aba) on one occasion mentioned the following: (It is worth noting that these are direct exhortations given by Huzoor (aba) to Ahmadi women).

"In this era Allah the Almighty has also enabled our Jama'at to benefit from modern forms of communication and the media. This is proving a great means of spreading the message of Islam far and wide. For example, through MTA the message of our Jama'at is reaching all corners of the world. However, this also increases our responsibilities because those who are hearing our message will also look in our direction to see if we are practicing what we preach. If they observe that the message we are conveying is true, but the standards of the Ahmadis themselves are weak, then instead of having a positive impact it may have the opposite [effect]. It is also possible that if others hear our message but feel that born Ahmadis are not living up to their required standards, they will take it upon themselves to spread the true teachings of Islam and live their lives accordingly. In that case the success and progress of our Jama'at, the Jama'at of the Promised Messiah (as), will be aligned to those pious newcomers and those left behind will be deprived of these blessings. Thus, do not let yourselves fall behind. Rather, seek to be at the forefront of conveying the truth of Ahmadiyyat, not only with your words, but with your conduct and deeds. Be the sources of light that illuminate the truth of Islam."

- Address at the National Ijtema Lajna Ima'illah UK Tilford, Surrey, UK 25 October 2015
- Published AlFazl International 25 March 2016

May Allah enable us to increase our capabilities to gain knowledge, do tabligh (propagation) and tarbiyyat (reformation) through maximum utilization of the latest inventions. May we excel in service and become Sultanan Naseera [strong helpers] of the Khalifa of the time and the proud progeny of Islam Ahmadiyyat. Ameen.

"…Allah the Exalted has given us a website for spiritual and educational programs of Jamā'at. We can only stay focused on it if we pay full attention to it. This will take us near to God and we will be saved from Satan."

(Friday Sermon delivered by Hazrat Khalifatul Masih V (aba) on 20 May 2016 at Gottenberg Mosque, Sweden)

Sources of English Translation used in Social Media Book:

Page Number in English Draft	Address/Sermon date and Occasion	Internet Link
9	*Address at the Annual Ijtema Khuddam ul Ahmadiyya UK 26 September 2016, Kingsley, Surrey*	Tariq Magazine Page 10 January 2017 VOL 21 ISSUE 1 http://www.tariqmagazine.org/wp-content/uploads/2017/02/TM_JAN_2017.pdf
22-23	*Address delivered at Annual Ijtema Lajna Ima'illah Germany 17 September 2011*	http://lajnausa.net/web/webfiles/*tarbiyyat/*Official%20Translation%20-%20Engish%20Translation%20Final%20-%20Address%20at%20Lajna%20Ijtima%20Germany%202011%20-%20V.1%2013.02.2014.pdf
32-33	*Message for Annual Ijtema Lajna Ima'illah Germany 10 July 2016*	Translation copied from Circular: Circular dated: 30.08.2017 London LS: 7585 Assistant Private Secretary (Honorary) Lajna Section: Posting Pictures of Lajna and Nasirat on Social Media
41-44	*Address to Khudam at Annual Ijtema UK 26 September 2016 Kingsley, Surrey*	Tariq Magazine Page 10 JANUARY 2017 VOL 21 ISSUE 1 http://www.tariqmagazine.org/wp-content/uploads/2017/02/TM_JAN_2017.pdf
51-54	*Friday Sermon Delivered 28 October 2016 at Baitul Islam Mosque, Toronto* *Published AlFazl International 18 November 2016*	https://www.alislam.org/library/books/Essence-of-Waqf-e-Nau.pdf
54	*Address at National Waqf-e-Nau Ijtema 28 February 2016 Baitul Futuh Mosque, London*	https://www.alislam.org/ismael/April-June-2016-EN.pdf Ismael Magazine Page 39 Apr-Jun 2016
55	*Address at National Waqf-e-Nau Ijtema 27 February 2016 Baitul Futuh Mosque, London*	https://www.alislam.org/ismael/Jan-Mar-2016-EN.pdf Published in Ismael Magazine page 46 Jan-Mar 2016

56	*Address at National Waqi-fat-e-Nau Ijtema 27 February 2016 Baitul Futuh Mosque, London*	Maryam magazine page 26 Apr-Jun 2016 https://www.alislam.org/maryam/Maryam-Apr-Jun-2016-EN.pdf
56	*Friday Sermon Delivered 28 October 2016 at Baitul Islam Mosque, Toronto*	https://www.alislam.org/library/books/Essence-of-Waqf-e-Nau.pdf
67	*Address at Annual Ijtema Lajna Ima'illah UK 25 October 2015*	http://lajnausa.net/web/webfiles/*tarbiyyat*/Huzoor's_Addresses_2015/OFFICIAL%20TRANSCRIPT%20-%20Address%20by%20Hazrat%20*Khalifa*tul%20Masih%20V%20%20at%20UK%20Lajna%20Ijtema%202015%20Version%203.pdf
70	*Address at Annual Ijtema Lajna Ima'illah Germany at Minhyme, Germany 17 September 2011*	http://lajnausa.net/web/webfiles/*tarbiyyat*/Official%20Translation%20-%20Engish%20Translation%20Final%20-%20Address%20at%20Lajna%20Ijtima%20Germany%202011%20-%20V.1%2013.02.2014.pdf
79-81	*National Waqfeen-e-Nau Ijtema UK 01 March 2015*	https://www.alislam.org/ismael/Jan-Mar-2016-EN.pdf Published in Ismael Magazine page 46Jan-Mar 2016
83	*Address at the Annual Ijtema Lajna Ima'illah Germany 17 September 2011*	http://lajnausa.net/web/webfiles/*tarbiyyat*/Official%20Translation%20-%20Engish%20Translation%20Final%20-%20Address%20at%20Lajna%20Ijtima%20Germany%202011%20-%20V.1%2013.02.2014.pdf
86	*Address at the National Ijtema Lajna Ima'illah UK Tilford, Surrey, UK 25 October 2015*	Official transcript of Huzoor's speech in English http://lajnausa.net/web/webfiles/*tarbiyyat*/Huzoor's_Addresses_2015/OFFICIAL%20TRANSCRIPT%20-%20Address%20by%20Hazrat%20*Khalifa*tul%20Masih%20V%20%20at%20UK%20Lajna%20Ijtema%202015%20Version%203.pdf